They Called Me Number One

THEY CALLED ME Number One

SECRETS AND
SURVIVAL AT
AN INDIAN
RESIDENTIAL
SCHOOL

BEV SELLARS

Talonbooks

© 2013 by Bev Sellars

Talonbooks
P.O. Box 2076, Vancouver, British Columbia, Canada V6B 3S3
www.talonbooks.com

Typeset in Electra
Printed and bound in Canada on 100% post-consumer recycled paper
Cover photograph by Scott Mack
Cover and interior design by Typesmith

First printing: 2013

The publisher gratefully acknowledges the financial support of the Canada Council for the Arts, the Government of Canada through the Canada Book Fund, and
the Province of British Columbia through the British Columbia Arts Council and
the Book Publishing Tax Credit for our publishing activities.

Library and Archives Canada Cataloguing in Publication

Sellars, Bev, 1955–
    They called me number one : secrets and survival at an Indian residential
school / Bev Sellars ; foreword by Hemas Kla-Lee-Lee-Kla (Bill Wilson) ;
afterword by Wendy Wickwire.

Includes bibliographical references and index.
Also issued in electronic format.
ISBN 978-0-88922-741-5

    1. Sellars, Bev, 1955–. 2. Sellars, Bev, 1955– —Family. 3. Shuswap
Indians—Education—British Columbia—Williams Lake—History.
4. Indians of North America—British Columbia—Residential schools.
5. Shuswap Indians—Biography. 6. Shuswap Indians—Crimes against.
7. St. Joseph's Mission (Williams Lake, B.C.)—History. I. Title.

E96.6.S154S44 2013   371.829'97943   C2013-901103-X

To my grandchildren, Orden Christopher Mack,
Kiara Jolene Mack, and Mya Druscilla Mack.
May you live full, unrestricted lives to fulfill the
potential I see in each of you

And to all the former students and their families
who attended residential schools in Canada,
the United States, and Australia

Contents

Foreword

In this book, Chief Bev Sellars shines light on one of the darkest periods in Canadian history. To me, the residential schools were horrific violations of humanity comparable to the Holocaust and based on the similarly ridiculous assumption that one race and its society are superior to all others. This wrong-headed thinking is the foundation upon which Department of Indian Affairs policy in Canada is based, and nowhere has this stupidity been expressed more blatantly than in the cesspool of mental, physical, and sexual abuse at the residential schools.

I am ashamed to admit that I knew little or nothing about Canada's Brown Holocaust until I was an adult. Thanks to the strength, vision, and wealth of my parents, I did not have to go to the religious prisons. The public school system and idyllic life of the Comox Valley isolated me from the horror and suffering of most Indians my age. I did notice that the kids from the local Indian reserve disappeared every September. I even acted as a driver to take three young relatives to the residential school in Port Alberni. Forgive me for I knew not what I did.

Despite the much-ballyhooed Canadian government apology for residential schools in June 2008, and the billions of dollars being spent on compensation and the Truth and Reconciliation Commission, few people know anything about the collaboration between church and state to destroy races of people and their cultures, a pursuit that lasted more than a hundred years in this "civilized" country. Genocide in the name of God was the policy that we supported whether we knew it or not.

Bev's story should be part of every school curriculum. All young Canadians need to be exposed to the truth of how generations of innocent children were abused. Such information will change Canadian Indian policy and prevent further atrocities.

My personal ignorance of "the schools" made it difficult for me to understand the reaction of even the strongest Indian leaders. I remember being inspired by the attitude, rhetoric, and even the oratory of some of my early heroes, only to see them wither in the face of White "authority," especially government or the churches. My family taught me to be proud of myself, to stand up for myself, and to look people in the eye when I am speaking to them. Meanwhile, nearly every Indian my age or older expressed shyness, nervousness, and a subservient attitude; I wondered where it came from. The answer now is obvious and is more clearly defined by the courageous writing of Chief Bev Sellars. I look forward to at least another book from Bev, a beautiful, talented, dedicated woman who has taught me so much.

Hemas Kla-Lee-Lee-Kla

(CHIEF BILL WILSON)

Preface

I was seventeen years old, desperate, and tired of trying to fit in. I was so young, yet I felt so worthless. All I could think of was to die. That night, years of abuse and put-downs finally caught up with me. A silly incident was the deciding factor. Although any one of much-worse experiences should have been the trigger, one small incident is all it took. That moment meant life or death, and I chose death. I saw no point in living.

Earlier that day, I had taken my mom's bottle of sleeping pills away from her because she had been drinking and had talked about taking *her* life. As unhappy as Mom's life was, I thought she still had reason to live. Now, I held those pills in my hand. I threw them in my mouth, swallowed easily, lay down in the bedroom, and waited to fall asleep. I did not think about others who were worse off than me. I did not think about the family and friends I would hurt. I just thought about how lost and lonely I felt and how desperately I wanted out of this world, a world that seemed to offer only intense unhappiness. It wasn't long before I felt myself going to sleep …

I started writing this book in the early 1990s when our communities first began to explore and deal with the aftermath of the Indian residential schools, in our case, St. Joseph's Mission in Williams Lake, British Columbia. I quickly changed my mind when a close relative angrily said to me, "I heard you are writing a book. Boy, you better not be writing about me!" This reaction caused me to reconsider making my – our – story public, but I continued putting my thoughts and memories on paper. In 2004, I decided to finish the book, even if it turned out to be only an historical record for my family. I asked myself, "Is it possible to make other people feel what I once felt and understand my message? Is it possible to make others realize the damage they are doing to themselves and to their loved ones? Is it possible to help others by writing about my experiences, or will it only create tension with others who shared those experiences? Should my memories stay just memories?"

I concluded that I had to write this book and share with those I know who are suffering the same experiences. In speaking with others, even those who went to residential school in other parts of Canada, I am amazed at how similar our stories are. I am amazed that the treatment of children was so consistently horrific all across Canada and the United States – even into Australia. It is as if the various churches running the schools all took the same training program based on abuse, neglect, and corporal punishment. Like other survivors of the residential schools, my experience resulted in a restricted world view, and the oppressive conditions under which I lived reduced my understanding of options available to me. In writing the book, I realized that I am still disassembling the restrictive world in which I once lived.

In the early 1990s, I went into the local shopping mall in Williams Lake. While there, I noticed a couple of women, fellow students from St. Joseph's Mission. I went over to say hello and eventually our conversation got around to my speaking out about the residential schools. One of the women said to me, "What pain have you suffered that qualifies you to speak on the schools?" I was surprised at her question. I don't remember my response.

How do you measure pain? The woman who asked that question was one of those whose home was completely broken because of alcoholism. Does that make her suffering more than mine? Or was my pain more because the comforts of growing up with caring grandparents meant I knew there was something better at home than the life and abuses we suffered at residential school? Does the fact that I chose not to become addicted to alcohol or drugs disqualify me from suffering? Or was my suffering more because I did not live life in a fog of alcohol and drugs? If I chose to live through it, deal with it, feel the full extent of the pain, and allow myself to grow emotionally and mentally, does that lessen my suffering?

Aboriginal people in Canada have a story to tell, a story most non-Aboriginals don't know about. Many Canadians are unaware of what happened in a country that proudly boasts of being one of the best places in the world to live; a supposedly democratic country where the freedoms and cultures of all are protected and respected. It is the greatest place to live for anyone, except for the original inhabitants of this land, the Aboriginal people.

I am angry about the way Aboriginal people have been and still are treated in Canada. I realize that complaining about the treatment of our people is justified, but doing something about it is more important. Writing this book has allowed me to grow. I found that I was not able to do anything to help my family, my community, and Aboriginal people in general until I learned to help myself.

I read somewhere that everyone is born with the potential for success, and it is only through life's experiences that we develop or destroy that potential. For many Aboriginal people, our most vulnerable and impressionable years, our childhood years, were spent at residential schools. Our mental, emotional, and spiritual growth was extremely stunted because of the way we were treated there.

"You have to tell our story like it is; don't hold back or make it seem like it wasn't as bad as it actually was. People have to know and believe what happened to us. That's what hurts ... when people don't believe what happened." That is what Charlie Gilbert from the

Williams Lake Indian Band at Sugar Cane said to me when I started speaking out about the residential schools and the damage done to our people. I cannot tell everyone's story. Others have told me some horrific stories about things that happened at residential schools, including a few potential murders, but they are not my stories to tell. I do not have the right to speak on behalf of other people, but my personal experience has exposed me to the effects the residential schools and other non-Aboriginal institutions have had on our society and our people. In this book, I do not speak on behalf of anyone else's experience unless it crossed with mine, and then I tell the story only from my perspective. The residential school and non-Aboriginal institutions had a drastic effect on me, and I am *eminently qualified* to speak on that.

Acknowledgements

I want to acknowledge my partner, Chief Bill Wilson, who, after reading the stories I wrote intended only for my family, encouraged me to turn them into a book for others. Bill also provided general editorial comments, as did my daughter Jacinda Mack.

I want to thank my son Scott Mack and his wife, Crystal Camille, for allowing me to use the photo of their beautiful daughters on the front cover of the book. If the residential school laws were still in place, at the age the picture was taken, the oldest would have already attended the school for four years and the youngest would have been there for two years.

I want to acknowledge all the former students of St. Joseph's Mission who filled in the blanks in some of my memories and allowed me to use their real names. Their support is greatly appreciated.

I want to say a special thank-you to Professor Wendy Wickwire and her husband, Professor Michael M'Gonigle, for their support. They encouraged me to reconsider my original plan to self-publish and introduced me to the good people at Talonbooks – Kevin Williams, Gregory Gibson, Ann-Marie Metten, Les Smith, and Daniel Zomparelli.

I would like to thank Elina Hill and Kristina Wray Baerg for providing me with constructive comments on my manuscript.

I also want to thank my family, my children, my brothers and sisters, nephews and nieces, and a few of my cousins for taking the time to read early drafts. As emotional as it was for some, they all encouraged me to make these stories public so they might help others. I would especially like to thank my brother Chuck Sellars for giving me the money to hire a professional editor, Brian Scrivener, to turn my stories into a manuscript that flowed.

I want to thank my grandparents for giving me the necessary grounding to make it through the difficult times in my life. I would also like to thank my mom, Evelyn Sellars, for reading and giving her nod of approval for the book. That was the deciding factor in taking it to a publisher.

Finally, thank you to all the ancestors on Turtle Island who continuously fought for our freedoms. We have survived the worst but our journey continues. We will carry on for all the grandchildren of every race.

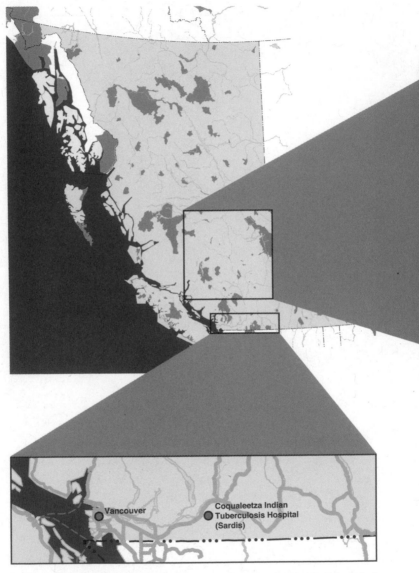

Coqualeetza Indian Tuberculosis Hospital (at Sardis, near present-day Chilliwack) had beds for 190 patients, with one building specifically for children. The average age of hospital patients was 16 years and the average hospital stay was 20 months.

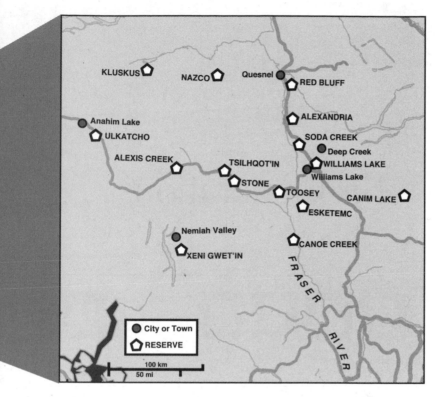

Map of First Nations Attending St. Joseph's Mission (Cariboo) Residential School
The St. Joseph's Mission (Cariboo) Residential School operated for nearly a century
on the Williams Lake First Nation lands. Official dates for the school are July 19, 1891,
to June 30, 1981. Students were drawn primarily from the fifteen First Nations in the
Cariboo Region, belonging to the Dakelh (Carrier), Secwepemc (Shuswap), and
Tsilhqot'in (Chilcotin) tribal councils. In addition, students were placed from across
the province, and included many other First Nations and Metis.

Six Generations

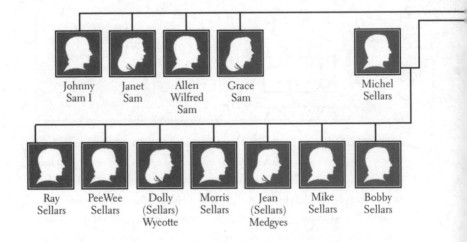

| Johnny Sam I | Janet Sam | Allen Wilfred Sam | Grace Sam | | Michel Sellars |

| Ray Sellars | PeeWee Sellars | Dolly (Sellars) Wycotte | Morris Sellars | Jean (Sellars) Medgyes | Mike Sellars | Bobby Sellars |

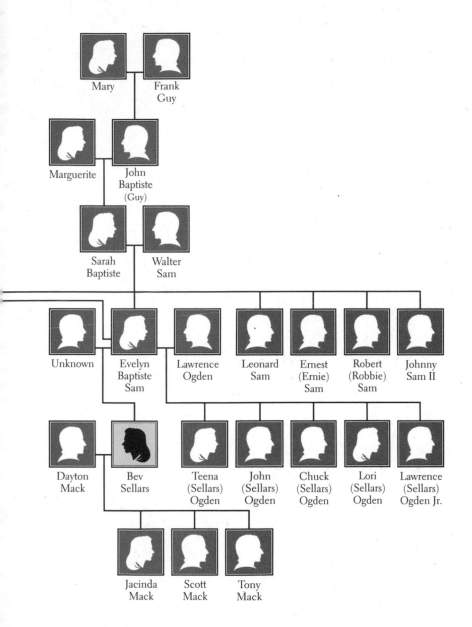

THEY
CALLED
ME
Number One

My Grandmother and Others Before Me

My grandmother Sarah (Baptiste) Sam was born July 29, 1896, in Marguerite, on the reserve of the most southerly Dakelh (Carrier) tribe. She grew up in the sagebrush hills around Marguerite, which is set on the banks of the Fraser River near Alexandria and north of Williams Lake. Her grandmother on her father's side originally came from Dakelh Territory farther north, in what is now known as the Quesnel area. Her grandmother on her mother's side came from Gitxsan-Wet'suwet'en Territory a little farther north, near Hazelton.

Gram's grandfather on her father's side was a Frenchman named François (Frank) Guy. In those days, Native people still travelled the Fraser River by canoe, and Aboriginal guides who knew how to navigate to any area in their territory and beyond were vital to newcomers like Gram's grandfather – people who could not make it in their own countries and so came looking for new opportunities. Without Aboriginal guides who supplied medicines, food, and transport, these newcomers would never have survived to "discover" the areas as quickly as they did.

In the late 1880s, Frank Guy fathered a baby, John, with an Aboriginal woman named Mary, but abandoned her and would not acknowledge the baby as his. John was Gram's dad. He grew up with his mother's people, raised by Old Twan with the surname Baptiste, instead of his father's name, Guy. John was summoned to his father's bedside when Frank was near death. Frank had no other relatives in Canada and he had done well for himself, owning most of Beaver Valley by

My grandmother's parents, John and Marguerite Baptiste.
Photo taken by C.D. Hoy in Barkerville circa 1909

the end of his life. He wanted to leave all his land and money to John, his only child. But John refused to go to Frank's bedside. He felt that since Frank had refused to acknowledge him earlier in life he wanted nothing to do with him on his deathbed. Frank's property was sold and all his money was sent to poor relatives in France. François Guy is buried in the cemetery at St. Joseph's Mission. His headstone reads:

Erected to the memory of François Guy of Beaver Lake, B.C.
Born at Crans, Ain, France, 1827
Died at 150 Mile House Cariboo, B.C.
– September 10, 1898
Generous to a fault and beloved by all who knew him

Until I found Frank's grave at the Mission, no one in my family knew that he was buried there.

As a young girl, Gram travelled the Fraser River by canoe even though she was deathly afraid of water. She viewed her fear of water as a failure of character and admired her older sister, Annie (Baptiste) Sellars, and her cousin Susan Twan, who confidently stood at the front of the canoe to paddle the wide and fast-moving river. She said, "I could never do that. I *sat* in the canoe and paddled!" Gram had many happy memories of her life "up home." She always considered Marguerite to be her home, even though she never lived there again after she married. Gram named my mom Evelyn Marguerite after the home she loved so much but had to leave behind.

Gram was seven years old when she first went to St. Joseph's Mission in 1903, and she spent the next nine years there with the month of July being the only time she was allowed home. During her fifth year at the Mission, her mother died. Gram felt sad that she could barely remember her mom even though she knew her mother Marguerite was a very special person to many people. Gram's mom knew all the Aboriginal medicines and would often be called when people were

My grandmother Sarah Sam and me on her hundredth birthday, July 29, 1996

sick. Marguerite died of smallpox after trying to cure others who had
the deadly disease. People tried to warn Marguerite to stay away from
those with smallpox, but Gram's mom had a big heart and she couldn't
stay away. She felt she had to try to help the people who were suffering.

Gram and her sister, Annie, were away from home at residential
school when their mother died. Gram's dad, John, went to the Mission
to get them but was told he would not be able to take his girls home
for the funeral. He would not give up, and finally he was allowed
to take Gram and Annie to their mother's funeral. Gram says that
lots of Marguerite's people paddled downriver from Quesnel for the
funeral. Gram says that many, many canoes lined the banks of the
river that day.

When Gram was eighteen years old, she married into a different
Aboriginal tribe. Her husband, Walter Sam, was Secwepemc (pronounced shi-HUEP-muh-k) or Shuswap. Her dad refused to attend
her wedding and told her, "I might as well be going to your funeral."
Her future mother-in-law, Sophie, did not agree with the marriage
either because, according to custom, she already had picked out a
Secwepemc girl for her son. At that time, arranged marriages were
the tradition, but by 1914, when Gram and Walter married, too much
interference from the outside was breaking that down.

Gram went to live with her husband's people after they married
and Walter's mother lived with them until she died. That was how
it was back then. Families were bigger and the grandparents were
always around to help. The problem was that Gram and Sophie did
not like each other. Gram did not have one good word to say about
her mother-in-law even though Sophie was an elder of the community
and the daughter of Buckskin, the chief of Soda Creek.

Aside from Sophie, Gram had patience with most people. She
looked after Sarah Jane, my grandfather's niece, who spent many years
in a mental institution. When she was not in the institution, she stayed
with Gram. Sarah Jane seemed to be in a world of her own most of
the time. She would talk and laugh to herself. My uncles tolerated

My mother, Evelyn Sellars, and my younger sister Teena Ogden, 1962 or '63

her, but she seemed to go out of her way to irritate them on purpose. She would raise a small dust cloud by sweeping the wood floor around them just as they sat down to eat. They would swear at her, but she just went on sweeping. It is a sad thing to say, but Gram was the only one who talked to Sarah Jane when she was living with us. Gram did not mind having her around.

From summer to winter, my grandparents went back and forth between our two communities. They had a house at Deep Creek (Cmetem). My grandparents also had a small house at Soda Creek (Xats'ūll) that we used when attending funerals or other community events and during the annual fishing season on the Fraser River. Although the community's main village was at Soda Creek, my grandparents' primary home was at Deep Creek. Because *Cmetem* in Secwepemc means "where the mountain meets the valley," and *Xats'ūll* means "on the edge" (because the village is on the banks of the Fraser River), I take joy in telling people that I have lived "on the edge" most of my life.

My mother, Evelyn, was Gram's fifth child, born April 20, 1925. She attended St. Joseph's Mission for ten years beginning in 1931 at age six. At age eighteen, Mom married Michel Sellars, who had also attended the residential school. Mom took Michel's last name and so became a Sellars just like her aunt Annie, who had married Michel's uncle. The Sellars name is common in the Soda Creek area, and everyone is related one way or another.

Before Mom and Michel had any children, they lived in Wells, where Michel worked. I have seen pictures of my mom when she was young, and she was an exceptionally beautiful woman; even in her old age, she is still a beautiful woman. While they were living in Wells, a Frenchman from the nearby village of Barkerville bragged to all his friends that he had a plan to get Michel and Mom drunk and "have his way" with Mom. One night, he invited Mom and Michel over for drinks and kept serving them booze. Mom poured hers away instead of drinking it. Michel, however, did not and he got drunk. The Frenchman told Michel to go lie down in the bedroom and even helped him get there. The Frenchman then proceeded to attack Mom. Michel must have heard Mom struggling and he woke up. He came out of the bedroom and he and the Frenchman began to wrestle. Mom ran out the door and headed back to Wells. On her way there, she passed a well-lit building and thought about going in but decided to keep going. As it turned out, that building was a police station and, if Mom had gone in, the police would have cleared her of any involvement in what happened after she left Michel and the Frenchman because, later that night when Michel got to Wells, he told Mom, "I think I killed that man." Michel convinced her to help him get rid of the body. Mom was not a willing accomplice, but Michel cut up the body and tried to burn the pieces. It did not work. They finally ended up burying the remains in the bush outside Wells. Eventually, the body was discovered, and it wasn't long before the Royal Canadian Mounted Police came looking for Mom and Michel because the Frenchman had told a few people in Barkerville that he was having them over that night.

Michel convinced Mom to take the blame for the murder because he said, as a woman, authorities would give her a lighter sentence. Mom was arrested for the murder but, as the investigation unfolded, it became clear that Michel was involved as well. Both went to jail to await trial. As a result, Mom's first child, Ray, was born in Oakalla Prison, the provincial penitentiary in New Westminster. My grandmother took Ray from the prison and raised him.

Six months later, after Mom and Michel were acquitted and released from jail, they continued their lives together at Soda Creek and had six more children. Because my mom was pregnant again with my brother PeeWee (James) shortly after getting out of jail, Gram kept Ray in her cabin at Deep Creek so Mom would not feel overburdened. I am sure Gram had grown attached to Ray and wanted to keep him anyway. Ray went to stay with Mom and Michel every now and again, and Gram had a good laugh at Ray one day. He came home from their place at Soda Creek and told Gram, "I don't like Evelyn's kids, they fight with me!"

Mom's life with Michel was hard. Michel drank, and all his demons came out when he was drinking. One time, Michel beat her up so badly that he did not recognize her the next morning. He looked at her and asked, "Is that you, Evelyn?" He did not remember beating her up. That morning, before Michel went to work, he pulled all the curtains closed and locked the doors so no one would see what he had done to Mom. Two weeks after the beating, the Indian agent came to visit the village and in his rounds went to see Mom. Even after two weeks, he still wanted to take Mom to the hospital. Beatings from Michel were regular, and Mom knew to have a spare pair of clothes and shoes hidden outside the door on Saturday night so that when he came home from drinking in Williams Lake, she could escape to her aunt Annie's house across the village.

Michel must have been a good father because my sister Jean only has good memories of him, as do my other older brothers and sister Dolly. I asked Mom once how Michel treated me as a baby, because it must have been obvious from my light skin that I was not his child. She said that he treated me well. Mom and Michel finally split for good when I was a year old. Mom took me and her other children to Gram's place and then went to look for work.

Gram said that after Mom left me at Deep Creek, I was always looking out the window for her. I don't remember that. My first memories are from times after she left me, when Gram was looking after me as a baby. I remember my grandmother leaning over me and changing my diaper. I also remember my brother Ray and Gram's son, my uncle Johnny, who were just a few years apart in age, teasing me, peeking in the window, trying to scare me. Gram looked over at them, said nothing, and continued to change my diaper. Maybe it was because Gram did not pay much attention to them that I remember not paying much attention to them either. The feeling I remember was one of contentment. I was at peace with the world, and I felt safe in Gram's old log house. I lived there until I was five years old, and that feeling of contentment is what I most associate with my grandparents and my community of Deep Creek.

My grandmother was fifty-nine years old when I was born. She was a short, plump woman but always had enough energy to take care of all the needs of her huge family. I am sure she got tired, but complaining was something she never did. She always wore one-piece dresses and long heavy stockings that tied above her knees. Gram wore pants only when she was going berry picking. The mosquitoes in the bush were thick and pants helped to protect her. Even when the temperature dipped to minus forty Fahrenheit, she wore dresses. Sometimes, if she was going to be outside for a long time in the extreme cold, she would put on a pair of pants under her dress. Her shoes were always well worn to one side. Her feet would swell on a regular basis, and the evening would usually find her soaking her feet in cool water. She always cut her own hair and kept it just above her neckline. Even though Gram's hands were muscular from the hard work she had done all her life, I remember her skin being soft. In her earlier years, she made buckskin gloves, moccasins, and occasionally a buckskin coat to earn a little extra money. Many times she sewed by candlelight late into the night. She blamed this for her poor eyesight later in life. She wore glasses and, before her eyes were too damaged from old age, she loved to read, usually romance stories.

Gram was a very clean woman and raised us to be the same. The fact that we did not have running water did not alter her rules of cleanliness. The creek was about a hundred yards from our house and we packed water from there. We had two aluminum buckets that we kept filled for drinking and cooking. Outside, we had an old oil barrel that we filled for laundry, dishes, and other cleaning purposes. Gram washed our wooden plank floors with boiling water on a regular basis.

She also cleaned our windows routinely with a white soap that dried on the glass before she rubbed them clean with a rag. She washed linen and clothes with a scrub board and hung them outside to dry.

On a regular basis, she would go through the house thoroughly to make sure there were no bedbugs. She boiled water and poured it along the edges of the mattresses. She made sure the swallows did not build their nests on our house because she believed that swallows transported bedbugs. My uncles and brothers would build birdhouses away from the house to encourage the birds to build their nests elsewhere. I remember a White man coming to our house and remarking how clean it was. At the time, I thought it was an unusual comment.

Gram was very mild mannered and I saw her get angry only a few times. Usually it was when she and my grandfather had gone into Williams Lake and my grandfather managed to sneak away to find some drinking buddies. My grandfather got loud when he was under the influence of alcohol, and Gram would get mad at him for being too loud in a public place. The only liquids Gram drank were water, coffee, and tea. She despised alcohol because she saw the destruction it caused to the ones she loved. She did not allow alcohol in her house. She constantly warned me about the dangers of alcohol while I was growing up. When my uncles would have pictures taken with them holding bottles of wine or beer in their hands, Gram would tell them mockingly, "I guess you think it makes you look good!"

Xp'e7e (pronounced "Ba'ah") is the Secwepemc word for "grandfather" and it is the name I always used for him. His English name – given to him by the priests in the community because priests or Indian agents always gave children their father's first name – was Walter Sam, son of Sam Kalkwett and Sophie.

Xp'e7e was tall and slim. He was a hard-working man. It was rare to see him relaxing. When we had company, he would sit and talk, but usually he was out working. We shared many times together outside near the barn or chicken house, with him shoeing the horses

Left to right: My Xp'eʔe, Walter Sam; Ernie Sam; their nephew Clifford Joe; Sarah Sam (Gram) with their sons Johnny II and Robbie; circa 1943. Clifford was in the army

or fixing their harness, and me sitting watching him or just playing close by. Many times there was no need for conversation. Like most people in our house, we did not speak unless there was something relevant to say. We did not make small talk or chatter on for nothing. The silence would eventually be broken by Xp'e7e telling me in the Secwepemc language, "Nūcwem, Pebbie?" (Isn't that right, Bevie?)

Xp'e7e's first language was Secwepemc and he spoke only broken English because he had not gone to residential school. In his broken English, Xp'e7e could not say "Bevie," the nickname everyone called me. When we were together, I would listen to Xp'e7e breathe in through his mouth and out through his nose. He always breathed that way. Thinking back on it now, it seemed like his breathing was laboured. When I think of Xp'e7e, that is the first thing I remember; then other memories of gentleness and strength come to mind. Xp'e7e always found it difficult to say no to me and my brothers Mike and Bobby. For example, Gram would not let us drink coffee, but Xp'e7e would let Bobby drink a cup of coffee with him if Bobby got up before Gram did. Sometimes he and Mike would get up early to have their time with Xp'e7e early in the morning.

Xp'e7e called Gram "Him." I don't think I ever heard Xp'e7e call Gram by her name, Sarah. Even when he was talking to someone about Gram, he would say "Him." Gram said that when we would go back to residential school at St. Joseph's Mission and Xp'e7e would be sleeping, he would call my name, "Pebbie." Xp'e7e and I never did have any deep conversations or even talk much, but we spent lots of quality time together.

I saw Xp'e7e angry twice. He was not violent but, on this particular day, we could hear the anger in his voice. It was the middle of the day and all of a sudden he started ordering Mike and Bobby to chop and pack in wood and he ordered me to pack water. I did what I was told and as Gram and I were going down to the creek to pack water I remember telling Gram, "Who does he think he is, the boss?" It was very out of character for Xp'e7e to give us orders. He always left that up to Gram. "Just keep quiet and do as you're told," Gram said. It was strange to see Xp'e7e mad.

The other time was when we were going out on the land. I can't remember exactly where it was but we were taking a route we had always taken. This time, though, a barbed-wire fence stretched across the path. Xp'e7e stopped the horses and got out of the wagon. He stomped around and swore a blue streak. We sat there for a while. Then he got back in the wagon, turned the horses around, and we went a different route. I did not realize what was happening at the time, but Xp'e7e was mad because of all the non-Aboriginals who were taking up land and fencing it off. At one time, Aboriginal people were free to harvest all the resources we needed to survive. There was a clash of cultures with the arrival of newcomers. It boiled down to the difference between attitudes towards the land. The Aboriginal attitude was that the land supplied you with everything you needed to survive and you could access it anywhere in your territory. With the newcomers came the notion of conquering the land and private property. Fences appeared where we had always gone freely before.

I wish now that Xp'e7e had cut that fence and just gone on our usual route, but he probably knew "the law" was against him. The Royal Canadian Mounted Police would have come and thrown him in jail for destruction of property or trespassing. The little freedoms we still had were coming to an end to accommodate all the newcomers to the land.

Xp'e7e had originally bought our old log house from a relative, George Evans Sr., for two cows and a calf. He moved it to Deep Creek and set it up. Living there when I was young were my grandparents; my uncles Ernie, Johnny, and Leonard; and my brothers Ray, Mike, and Bobby. My sister Jean was there with me for a short while and then she left. My brothers Morris and PeeWee were there sometimes too. We did not all stay there at the same time. People would come and go, and there was no question about them staying anywhere else. My grandparents' small log house at Deep Creek was home base for every-one. Usually, the only time we were all there together was Christmas. All my older brothers and sisters stayed at our grandparents' house at one point in their childhoods, but eventually most of them left and went their own way.

It is funny to think that despite being born in prison, my brother Ray was always hunting, trapping, or doing something outside. Ray's nickname was "Ray Boone" after Daniel Boone, who supposedly was the ultimate outdoorsman, at least, he was in that show on TV. When Ray was home, he would take our horse Loco and be gone all day. Sometimes he wouldn't get back until late at night, and my uncles and Gram would stay up and wait for him. Some worry was involved if he was late. Then all of a sudden a small fire would light up somewhere on the mountain by our place. "There he is!" someone would say and sure enough a short while later we would hear the horse clomping into the yard.

Ray's initials are carved all over the territory. Wherever he would go he would initial "RS" or "Ray" into the trees. He was very proud of the fact that he put his mark wherever he went in the territory. During the winter, Ray would trap on Xp'e7e's trapline. Our house was usually filled with stretching frames covered in furs of every sort. Ray trapped mink, beaver, lynx, weasel, squirrels, and every once in a while a fox. I am sure with all those stretched pelts in the house it must have smelled awful to some people, but I never noticed. Ray sometimes stank of beaver castor, the oil with a distinct musk odour that comes from the animal's scent glands. Before he went trapping, Ray would remove his human scent from the traps by boiling them. He would then rub beaver castor on his hands before he handled the boiled traps. Sometimes I went with him to check his traps that were close to the house. It was always a special treat for me to hang around with Ray. He took good care of me. We would trudge over frozen ponds and creeks to where he had set his traps. Even though sometimes it was bitterly cold, we dressed for the weather and enjoyed ourselves out in the bush.

I always wanted to go hunting with Ray but he would never let me. Once he had my favourite horse tied outside the house and was getting his gun and gear ready to go hunting. I went outside and jumped on Loco's back. When Ray came out, he tried to get me off the horse but I would not budge. I was determined to go hunting with him. Annoyed, he told me, "Okay then, go get your coat!" I said, "No, you go get it." I knew that if I got off the horse he would leave me. Muttering under his breath, he went and got my coat. "Here, put it on!" he barked when he came back. Even though I knew he was mad at me, I had a big smile on my face. Ray jumped on Loco and away we went. We went for about a mile or so behind the house and headed home. "Nothing around today," he said. We got to the house, and Ray helped me down from the horse. He said he was going to go take the saddle off in the barn. I went into the house, but Ray did not join me. When I went to check, he was gone. He had tricked me and now Ray was gone on his hunting trip!

I watched Ray and others gut and skin many moose and deer. While Ray was skinning a deer he would cut off chunks of raw meat and eat them. He offered me some, but I always said no, and he would laugh.

When it got too crowded at Deep Creek, my uncle Leonard sometimes moved to the house at Soda Creek. He was a quiet man, a thinker, who always had books to read: medical books, novels, crime-scene investigations, and martial-arts books. When I was about ten years old, he tried to teach me how to defend myself but gave up after a few lessons. I wasn't interested, even though he continuously stressed the importance of it. He wanted me to be prepared if I ever got into a situation with a White man. There were plenty of non-Aboriginal men in the area who forced their violence on Aboriginal women and went unapprehended and unconvicted. Leonard wanted me to be able to defend myself. Unlike his brothers, Leonard was short and stocky. I am told he was tough although I never saw him fight. His brothers were scared of him, and Gram used that fear when one of them came back drunk and making a ruckus. All Gram had to say was, "Leonard's upstairs!" and they immediately settled down, whether he was there or not.

"Upstairs" was the wide-open space where most of us slept. Only Xp'e7e and Gram had an enclosed room downstairs. My grandparents tried every way to save a few pennies. Coal oil cost money, so our coal-oil lamp was not lit until it was fairly dark and then it was on only for a short while before everyone was ready to go to bed. It was always early to bed and up early the next morning to the smell of breakfast waiting downstairs. On nights that I couldn't sleep, I would look over to Uncle Leonard's bed and watch the glow of his cigarette. My uncle Leonard smoked a lot and, before he went to bed, he would roll fifteen to twenty cigarettes; by morning they would all be gone. My "counting sheep" exercise on nights when I couldn't sleep was to watch Leonard's cigarettes glow bright each time he took a puff. I would then entertain myself by guessing how many more puffs he would take before he needed to light another one.

My uncles and brother Ray would usually leave in the spring to look for work. They would take jobs that were available locally, but sometimes they had go to the United States to find work in the fruit orchards. In the late 1960s and early 1970s, orchard owners would hire buses to come and round up Native people to work for them. Entire families from Soda Creek and other Native communities would move for the summer to pick fruit in the Okanagan or the United States. Gram would say in the fall, just before we went back to the Mission, "The grasshoppers should be home soon." By "grasshoppers," she was referring to anyone who was away. They were here and there, jumping around looking for work during the summer then would return in the fall. I think this was a term commonly used for Aboriginal people because I have heard others call their relatives "grasshoppers" too. In the fall, my uncle Ernie and my brother Ray were in demand to be guides at hunting lodges for hunters who came from all over the world looking for bear, moose, deer, or elk. At Christmas, they would get cards from various countries in Europe and from cities across the United States. I was impressed that the little cards came from such faraway places. Years after my brother Ray died, Christmas cards still arrived from the same people in Sweden and Denmark.

Xp'e7e would take a man named London hunting every year. London was from Vancouver and either worked in or owned a hotel. I don't think it was a high-class hotel; he did not stand out as being rich. I don't know what London paid Xp'e7e for taking him out hunting, but Xp'e7e looked forward to London coming every year. I think he liked London because, for a few days, Gram was not around and he was free to drink liquor with London on their hunting trips.

London would pay Mike, Bobby, and me five dollars to share, a gold mine to us, to take the horses up to Forest Lake, a distance of about five miles. Gram did not mind London, and sometimes he brought material with him that she sewed into blankets for our beds. Gram did not like all the "junk" he brought from the hotel. London would bring items that people had left behind in the hotel. Gram would not allow any of the stuff into the house until she had boiled it in a big tub outside. She would then take the buttons and zippers off the clothes and put them away. She separated the clothes she could make blankets from and burned the rest, which was most of the stuff London brought. After I had grown up, I went to look for our home in the woods at Deep Creek. All that was left of the log house was the foundation. It amazed me to see how small it was. It further amazed me to think that it was *never* too small to accommodate all those who happened to be around at the time. Everyone came, went, and got along without interfering in each other's lives. The kids would sleep on the floor when the beds were full, but it never bothered us. We were always comfortable. Gram made soft mattresses out of old denim filled with hay. Whenever someone shot a duck or goose for our meal, Gram collected the down feathers and, when she had enough, she made pillows. For blankets, Gram used material she collected from various sources, including from our friend London.

Life at Deep Creek was very good. I knew I was safe. Gram, Xp'e7e, my uncles, and my brothers Ray and Mike were very protective of me. We were not spoiled with material things. We never had store-bought toys. Gram made us whistles from wood, and any other toys that we had, our uncles made or we made ourselves. We did not have expensive furniture. We had a tattered plastic couch, plain plywood on the walls and wooden plank floors. The only things on the wall were a few pictures of the family and some religious items, such as statues of the Virgin Mary that the kids had won for good grades or good behaviour. While I was growing up I never thought of us as "poor," but I am sure others did. We might not have had many material things but we had more than any amount of money could buy. We were part of a family that loved us and provided for all our needs.

CHAPTER 2

Sardis
Hospital
=
Loneliness

Gram said that when I was five years old I became very sick. I would not eat and I did not have energy to do anything. She knew something was wrong because I just lay on the bed all day. The Indian nurse said that I had tuberculosis. So on November 17, 1960, I was admitted into the Coqualeetza hospital in Sardis, outside Vancouver – more than two hundred miles south of my home. I stayed there for the next twenty months.

I have many memories of Sardis, including the vivid memory of standing at the window in the hospital and looking out in different directions wondering which way was home. I wondered if I would ever return there or whether I was going to be in hospital forever. I was very lonely. I had lost my whole family.

The ward I stayed in on the hospital's second floor was divided in two: one side for the older girls and the other side, where I was, for the younger girls. There were about fifteen beds on each side of a partition made of wood panelling and glass. The nurse's station was right outside our ward. The boys' ward was on the other side of the nurses' station. The adults were on the floor above us, and the doctors' offices were on the fourth floor. A TV set was mounted on the wall on the older girls' side. The older girls wouldn't let us sit on their beds while we watched TV unless a nurse was around. On the weekends, we watched cartoons in the morning, played outside on nice days, and went to school in Occupational Training (O.T.) on the third floor. O.T. was a place where patients made wallets, belts, and other crafts.

The staff came, did their jobs, and left, except for Miss Costello, a nurse with short, wavy blonde hair. Miss Costello was kind to me and other patients. She was a real comfort to me when I was very lonely and needed someone to latch on to. Her words were kind and she seemed genuinely to care about me and the other children. She treated us as if we mattered to her. Miss Costello's kindness meant the world to me, and she is still the only happy memory I have of Sardis. Miss Costello took us on walks outside the hospital buildings, and I have always loved the smell of freshly cut grass because I associate it with Miss Costello. Her time with us was special. I admired her, and right then and there I decided I wanted to become a nurse just like her when I grew up.

Miss Costello's complete opposite was Miss Pentecost, a short, red-haired nurse with a temper to match the colour of her hair. We were always careful not to upset Miss Pentecost when she was on shift. I also had to go to the fourth floor quite often to see the doctor. I remember his office was somewhat dark and I had to climb up on a big armchair. I was given needles frequently, so many that later, when I attended St. Joseph's Mission, the other kids would ask about the needle marks on my arms. I also remember having to swallow a narrow, yellowish rubber tube on a regular basis. The doctor would pull it back out slowly once I managed to swallow it so far. It was awful enough trying to swallow the darn thing, but having it pulled back out of my throat was very unpleasant and sometimes quite painful. I don't know why I had to swallow that tube because no one ever gave me a reason. All I know is that I have always suffered from throat problems and I suspect there is a connection to the tube I had to swallow so frequently as a child.

Some of my other memories of Sardis are of rain all the time, playing hopscotch beside the laundry building, making pretend soup out of candy and water, and wanting to be old enough so that I could go with Miss Costello when she gave the older girls cooking lessons in the shacks across from the hospital. I also remember a very tall female teacher getting mad at me because I could not make a sentence fit all on one line. She grabbed my pencil and angrily said, "Look, my writing is bigger than yours. I can make it fit on one line, why can't you?" I was sitting at the end of a long table, and the other kids at the table were looking at me. I felt hurt, ashamed, and extremely frustrated that I was unable to do something that seemed so simple.

Sometimes I had visitors at the hospital. My brother Ray said he came to visit me, but I have no memory of that. My uncle Ernie told me later in life that he had come to visit me. The nurse brought me out from the ward and Ernie stood there trying to get me to come to him. I cried and wanted to go back to the ward. That would have been Uncle Ernie and I must have hurt his feelings by not wanting to visit with him.

My mom and her new common-law husband, Lawrence Ogden, came to visit me while I was at Coqualeetza. I remember the visit, although at the time I did not know who they were. I had forgotten Mom because I had been with Gram since I was a year old. I do remember, though, that Mom and Lawrence took me out for ice cream. They put me in the middle of the back seat of their car and I stared at the backs of their heads. The car seemed huge. Mom rested her left arm on the top of the front seat, and she would turn around and talk to me every once in a while. Mom told me years later that they had come to the coast because Lawrence wanted to buy a car in Vancouver and they thought they would stop by to see me on their way home.

My worst memory of Sardis is that Miss Costello got married and left the ward. I don't know if she moved somewhere with her new husband or just quit work. All I know is that I felt extremely lonely and depressed when I realized she was gone for good. The pain that I felt when I realized she was not coming back is one of the big hurts in my life and another severe blow. Miss Costello didn't even tell me goodbye. All I knew was that she was gone and I only found out after she had left.

Before I left Sardis, a nurse took me shopping in one of the local clothing stores. She and the sales clerk picked out different clothes for me, and kept asking what colour clothes I wanted. I always answered, "Blue." One nurse said to the other, "Either blue is her favourite colour or that's the only colour she knows." That remark made me angry. I did not want them thinking I was so dumb that I didn't know any other colours, so I said, "Blue is my favourite colour." They laughed at me, and I got embarrassed and blushed with shame. Blushing is a curse that has plagued me my whole life but the first time I remember experiencing it was at Sardis. There, at a very young age, I learned to be ashamed of the smallest things and, even though I blushed less as I got older, I have never quite gotten over it.

On July 10, 1962, a couple came to pick me up from the hospital. I remember an older woman telling me she was taking me home. I told her she was fat. She laughed, and I got the impression she was a kind woman, so I was willing to go home with her. That was Gram, my grandmother. She would have been sixty-six years old at the time. She and my grandfather Xp'e7e had travelled down to Sardis by Greyhound bus. Even though it had only been twenty months since I had seen them, I did not remember them. I am sure I had blocked them from my memory to try to dull the pain of loneliness I felt from missing them.

I was seven years old when I returned home from my stay at Sardis. I had forgotten my family and it took me a while to put the right name to the right person. Everyone seemed happy to have me around them. One of the first things they made me do when I got home from Sardis was have a foot race with my brother Bobby, who was two years older than me. They wanted to see how strong I was. I was eager to please, so I happily took part. We ran from the old log house to a gate about a hundred yards away and back. I ran as fast as I could, but Bobby beat me. Everybody had a good laugh. I still remember the feeling of my body trembling from the race but I also remember feeling intensely happy that I was home again.

Not long after I got back from Sardis, I had to go to the hospital again, this time in Williams Lake. I had gone fishing with Bobby and Mike a short distance from our house. Mike was casting his fishing hook into the creek when the hook got caught on the back of my calf. The barb went right through the skin. Of course, I cried. Mike helped me back to the house, where Gram and Xp'e7e really gave him heck for hooking me. But Mike was always my big protector and I'm sure he did not mean to hook me. I still feel bad for Mike because of the big tongue-lashing Gram and Xp'e7e gave him.

I guess they overreacted because I had just gotten back from Sardis. Instead of trying to get the hook out of my leg themselves, Xp'e7e picked me up, packed me the mile or so to the highway, hitched a ride into town, and took me to the hospital. Once the hook was removed from my leg, only a small bandage was needed to cover it. But Xp'e7e packed me all the way back to the highway. We hitched another ride out to Deep Creek, and then he packed me all the way from the highway to the house. I could have walked, but Xp'e7e packed me all that way.

CHAPTER 3

St. Joseph's Mission

=

Prison

Three weeks after I got back from Sardis, I left home for St. Joseph's Mission. Like other Aboriginal, Inuit, and Metis children across Canada, I was required by Canadian law to attend residential school from age seven to sixteen, although some were younger than seven when they arrived at the school and others were older than sixteen when they left. I lived at St. Joseph's from September 1962 to June 1967. The Mission was run by the Oblates of Mary Immaculate and set in an isolated valley approximately ten miles south of the town of Williams Lake. The school was only twenty-five miles from my home community, but it may as well have been a million. The kids from Williams Lake Indian Band were only five miles from home, and yet they still did not see their families for ten months of the year.

About a mile and a half before we got to the school there was a hill with a full view of what is now called the San Jose Valley. It was there that we got our first glimpse of the Mission buildings. The largest building was a rectangular four-storey structure. Half of it housed the boys and the other half housed the girls. At each end of the basement were playrooms – large empty rooms with concrete floors covered in a thin layer of linoleum. Lockers lined the walls and a TV set in one corner had a couple of wooden benches in front of it. Between the boys' and girls' playrooms were the dining rooms and kitchen, with the laundry room behind. Nearby dining rooms for the priests and brothers, sisters, teachers, and supervisors were enclosed so they had privacy for their meals. The more than three hundred children ate together in an open space with the boys on their side and the girls on the other. Workmen ate in an open space at one end of the boys' dining room.

The next floor up housed the senior girls' and boys' dorms at opposite ends of the building. Between them were several other rooms. There was a sewing room, which also served as the infirmary. Sister Superior's room was at one side and Father O'Connor's room – the principal's room – was on the other. Right at the centre was the main office and a little parlour where people visited. The chapel was on the second floor as well, directly above the laundry room on the first floor.

The junior and intermediate dorms were on the third floor, and bedrooms for all the nuns, priests, brothers, some of the teachers, supervisors, and everyone else except the workmen were on the fourth floor. The workmen had a bunkhouse away from the main building. There were also a few houses where some of the teachers and maintenance people stayed with their families.

Stairways at each end of the building had huge iron doors that clanged when they shut. The dorms had the bare necessities: beds and curtains. We slept on thin, narrow mattresses on single beds. In my mom's and Gram's generations, they slept on mattresses made out of flour sacks stuffed with straw. Each child had to go to the barn and fill their flour sack with straw. Mom laughs when she talks about that. She says the kids would stuff their flour sack until they couldn't fill it anymore, and then during the night you would hear, "Plop," and a little while later, "Plop," and this went on throughout the night. Their mattresses were so rounded from stuffing them too full that the kids would roll off during the night. Mom says they changed the straw once a year and they washed their sheets once a month.

When the weather turned cold in the winter, the Oblates had a hard time heating the buildings. During the years my mom was at the Mission, often the dormitory was a few degrees below freezing during the night. Later in life and because of her memories of the cold dormitory in the night, Mom always made sure any kids in the house had extra blankets. She said she knew how awful it was to be cold at night.

When it was time for us to go to the Mission, a priest would come pick us up in our community. Sometimes, though, my grandmother would take us to the highway to catch the Greyhound bus into Williams Lake. From there a priest would pick us up and take us to the Mission. Fortunately, I was not one of the many children who were loaded into the backs of cattle trucks and brought back to the Mission that way.

No one asked our parents or grandparents if they wanted their children to attend the school. Gram always said to Mike, Bobby, and me, "I sure hate to send you kids back to the Mission but, if I don't, they will put me in jail." Gram knew that this was no idle threat. Others in our area had been sent to jail because they would not surrender their children. After I had children of my own, and especially as they approached the age when they would have been taken away from me, I realized the heartache that sending us away must have caused Gram, Mom, and others. I would have moved to the ends of the earth to avoid having my kids taken from me. Taking my kids away would have been the worst thing anyone could have done to me. It would have left me emotionally crippled and, as many parents did, I might have tried to ease the pain and guilt with drugs or booze. Even though children had no choice but to attend the schools, many parents felt guilty because they knew the abuses their children would have to endure. As parents, they were powerless to do anything about it.

Once we got to the schools, the routine was the same year after year. Our personal belongings were taken away and placed in an attic, and we were not allowed to touch them again until we went home. We were supplied with everyday clothing, underwear, jeans, a shirt, socks, and shoes, and we were placed in a junior, intermediate, or senior group. The first year I attended, I was put in the junior girls' group because

I was only seven years old. There were seventy-two of us in the junior girls' dorm.

Our hair was cut and we were "deloused" with the pesticide DDT. The older girls were in charge of doing the younger ones. Even though we held a towel over our faces, some of the DDT fell after we took the towel away and it stung our eyes and tasted awful. Anne (Michel) Stinson, a girl from my community who was a year or so older than me, remembers trying not to put too much DDT on one girl's hair. The nun grabbed the can of pesticide away from her and proceeded to pour heavy amounts of it on the girl's head. Anne was told to do all the girls' hair that way. In the early 1970s, DDT was banned in Canada because it was proven harmful to animals. And even though they used DDT on us at the Mission, many times I went home in the summer or at Christmas with bugs in my hair. The first thing Gram would do was clean my hair – but without the DDT. She picked out the nits (eggs) with her hands. I was always bug-free when I went back to the Mission, but I had to endure the DDT anyway.

Another thing that happened soon after we arrived at residential school is that we were given a number that would become our identity throughout our years at school. I became Number 1 on the girls' side. Although the other kids all continued to call me by name, "Bev Sellars" ceased to exist for most of the nuns and priests. Instead they would say, "Number 1, come here" or "I want these girls in my office, Numbers 3, 14, 72, and 105" or "Number 1, say the second decade of the rosary." Ninety or more years after she left St. Joseph's Mission, my grandmother still remembered her number – 27 – and – 28 – the number assigned to her sister Annie. My mom remembers her number was 71. Thankfully, our numbers were not tattooed on our skin.

My first morning at St. Joseph's Mission was memorable: I woke up to the nerve-racking sound of a nun loudly clapping her hands. My immediate obedience was quickly established. Along with the other girls, I learned to jump out of bed as soon as the clapping started, otherwise we were hit with the strap – a strip of leather cut from a conveyor belt. We scrambled out of bed to avoid it, and as soon as we were out, the nuns insisted that we make the bed just so – corners tight, sheets straight and smooth.

We then lined up two by two. Anyone who had wet the bed had to strip the sheets and then stand in a second line. As hard as I tried to have an empty bladder before I went to bed, many times I was one of the girls in that line. We were told we were too lazy to get up and go to the bathroom and our punishment was the strap. In addition, the nuns ridiculed us for wetting the bed and thus gave other kids reason to torture us with taunts. At least I did not have to wear a sign on my back that read "Bed Wetter" the way some of the boys did.

At home, Gram made me go to the bathroom at night before I went to bed and limited the water I drank in the evening. Then she would fix my bed to ensure that just the sheets got wet. She was never angry with me for wetting the bed, and she never ridiculed me. It was quite different at the Mission. There were times I tried to hide the fact that I had wet the bed. I did not want to get the strap. I had never been beaten before and was traumatized the first few times the leather hit my skin, but that became our morning ritual and, in time, it became less of a shock. It still hurt like heck, but I knew to expect it.

The junior and intermediate girls' dorms on the third floor all shared one bathroom, which had only five or six toilet stalls and one shower room. The shower room had no stalls, just bare shower heads. The junior girls showered on some days, and the intermediate girls showered on other days. We were required to shower with our underclothes on. After we had showered, we were given dry underclothes and had to go into a private toilet stall to change.

After I had showered and dressed on my first morning at the Mission, I, along with six or seven junior girls, was told to go and clean

up the schoolyard. The yard looked huge to me as a seven-year-old –
it was probably two to three acres. I was hungry and wanted to go to
breakfast, so we tried to hurry. The other girls and I filled our bags with
as much garbage as we could find and ran back to the building. The
nun got very angry and sent us back outside, and we picked up garbage
until the yard was spic-and-span. She came out and did a thorough
inspection. By the time we were allowed to go inside, we had missed
breakfast because we had taken too long to clean the yard.

When I first started at the Mission, I had an older sister, Jean, at the
school, but she was in the senior girls' dorm and almost a stranger to
me. I had three brothers there too but I only knew Bobby and Mike.
My older brother Morris was a stranger to me because I saw my older
siblings only at Christmas and in the summer. I didn't get to know
Jean, Morris, or PeeWee until I left the school. My older sister Dolly
was employed at the Mission for the first couple of years while I was
there and would visit me in the playroom.

I grew up very quickly at the school. I was not much more than a
baby, but to most of the adults in charge, it was unacceptable for me to
respond like a normal child. My mom remembers that at the beginning
of each year, some of the younger boys would see their older sisters
up close in church and seek a bit of comfort by trying to go sit with
them, only to be yanked back onto the boys' side of the church. I felt
bad for the kids who would cry at night because it was their first time
away from home. They were lonely for their families and couldn't go
to their siblings even if they were in the same dorm. The nun would
warn them that if they did not stop crying, they would get the strap.
It did not take long for the new kids to learn to bury their feelings no
matter how scared or lonely they felt. It took the nuns only two or three
nights to stop the crying. After that, the dorm was quiet when the lights
were out. I didn't cry. Even though I was only seven years old, I was well
acquainted with the feeling of loneliness. I had learned to suppress it
while in hospital at Coqualeetza.

In residential school, we always lined up two by two – walks, church, meals, school, confession – always two by two. On weekday mornings, after we had finished our chores, we lined up to go to the two-storey school building, which was about seventy-five yards from the main building. Grades one, two, three, and four were downstairs and grades five, six, and seven were upstairs. The kindergarten class was in the main building.

After we were herded into the building on the first morning in September, the teachers stood outside the classroom directing the kids where to go. My first year at school, I headed for the grade-three room along with the other grade-three kids when Miss Durfeld, the grade-two teacher, pulled me out of the line. "You're in my class," she said. "No, I'm in grade three," I told her. She didn't believe me and tried to force me into her classroom. I resisted. Thankfully, I had not been at the school long enough to know that I should blindly obey everything I was told to do. Miss Norris, the grade-three teacher, came out to see what the commotion in the hallway was all about. Miss Durfeld told her I thought I was in grade three, but she knew I should be in her class. Miss Norris said, "No, she's right. The sister gave me her report card and she is assigned to grade three." I was so thankful to Miss Norris for rescuing me.

Miss Durfeld made an honest mistake. I had completed grades one and two in Sardis, but I was at least two years younger than everyone else in my class. If everyone were assigned by age, I really should have been in grade two, but that's not how it worked at the Mission. It was common to have a mix of ages in one grade. My brother Mike was four years older than me, and Bobby, two years older, but they were both in grade three with me. My sister Dolly, who was six years old when she went to the Mission, was in grade one with my two oldest brothers: Ray, who would have been ten, and PeeWee, who would have been eight years old. My uncle Johnny was also in the same class, and he would have been twelve years old. The reason for the range of ages was that some students didn't start school until the Department of

Indian Affairs and the churches had finally caught up with them and got strict about getting them to enrol. School authorities were paid per child and they needed the money, so they rounded up as many Indian children as they could find, even though some of them were already ten or eleven years old.

Miss Norris, my grade-three teacher, was good to all the kids. I remember her as being firm but not mean; then again Annie Michel and I were her pets, so our experience was probably different than that of other kids in the class. I looked forward to going to Miss Norris's class because it was such a relief to get away from the nuns. I also liked Miss Norris's class because she kept books in the cloakroom and would allow us to take them to read. Unfortunately, she lasted only a year before going back to England. The good teachers did not stay long.

I remember little incidents that happened in grade three. I remember where I sat and where my brothers sat. I remember being frustrated because I couldn't write properly. In frustration I scribbled on my paper, and Miss Norris scolded me. I remember teachers from every year at the Mission except grade four. In grade five, I did not learn how to spell my teacher's name, but it sounded like "Miss Poulevard." She was middle-aged, slim, and brown-haired. She kept her distance from any personal involvement with the kids except when she got mad; then she would scream at us. Miss Poulevard always wore a light sweater over her blouse but never put her arms through the sleeves, although she always did up the top button. Every afternoon after lunch, she read us a chapter from a book. She read stories like *Rin Tin Tin*, *The Hardy Boys*, *Nancy Drew*, and others. Those afternoon stories were the highlight of my grade-five year. I hated Fridays because we had to wait until Monday after lunch before she would read us another chapter.

Grade six was a painful year for all the students in Miss Bouchemay's class. She was just plain mean. Miss Bouchemay was an older spinster, overweight, and with one leg shorter than the other. The shoe on her short leg had a sole that was probably six or seven inches thick. She was always sucking on a cough drop. One of the other girls told

me it was because she drank a lot and used cough drops to cover the
smell of the alcohol. Miss Bouchemay also used lots of face powder,
red lipstick that stuck to her teeth, rouge on her cheeks, and perfume
that made my stomach turn. She always wore her hair in a bun on the
back of her head. Her buckteeth had small gaps between them and
she would spit when she talked.

Whenever someone would do something Miss Bouchemay did
not approve of, she would say from the front of the room, "If I have to
come down there, *you'll pay* for my steps." Jim Lulua from Nemiah
Valley and Willie Alec from Nazko were the rebels in the class. They,
especially, paid for her steps many times. The school must have had
a special budget for the yardsticks she broke on the kids. Patience was
definitely not one of her virtues.

Every day after class, Miss Bouchemay would make one of the
girls stay to help her walk back to the main building. We all hated
that job, but we each had to take our turn doing it. Rose Sellars and I
also had to take organ lessons from her so we could play the organ in
church. Rose played better than me so, after a few lessons where my
fingers were constantly whacked with a ruler for making mistakes, I
was given my walking papers. That made me extremely happy but on
a regular basis Rose would come back from organ lessons with swollen
fingers. We could also tell that she had been crying.

It was in Miss Bouchemay's grade-six class that we finally learned
to tell time. Every evening, the nun would send one of us down to the
main floor outside the chapel to check the time. I had been down to
check the clock many times and I knew the routine. "The big hand is
on the nine and the little hand is on the eight," or whatever time it was.
One night I went down and, instead of telling the nun the position of
the clock hands, I told her what time it was. She looked at me with total
disgust and sent me back downstairs again. "I told you to see where the
hands were!" she barked. After that, I questioned whether I could tell
time. I learned that speaking my mind or questioning anything would
only get me into trouble. Using my mind was even more unacceptable.

We were more like robots than normal children. Our lives were decided for us – twenty-four hours a day. "Yes, Sister" and "Yes, Father" were the limit of our conversations with school authorities. By the time we hit grade six, Miss Bouchemay was shocked that no one seemed to know how to tell time. She said that was something we should have known by grade two. I felt dumb when I thought I knew how to tell time and the nun made me question myself, and I felt dumb that I didn't know how to do something I should have known at least four years earlier.

It was also in Miss Bouchemay's class that an incident happened which made me ashamed for years afterwards. Class was almost finished for the day, and I needed to go to the bathroom. I raised my hand to let Miss Bouchemay know, but she said I could wait. I really needed to go but, as long as I was sitting down, I knew I could keep from wetting myself. However, at the end of every school day, we had to kneel and say a prayer before we went back to the main building. I knew I was in trouble as soon as I knelt down. I raised my hand again, but Miss Bouchemay gave me a look that I knew meant "Keep quiet or else." I didn't dare ask again. We were halfway through the prayer, and I couldn't hold myself anymore. I could feel my leg getting wet and a pool forming around my knees. I was never so embarrassed in my life. Of course, some of the kids in class enjoyed my embarrassment and made a point of spreading the word around the school about what happened to me. On the other hand, Doreen (Paul) Johnson, who sat behind me, went and got some paper towel and wiped up the pool of urine for me. She helped me up and took me to the bathroom, rinsed my panties, and cleaned me up before we went back to the main building. Moments of tenderness when you need it most are not forgotten. Miss Bouchemay saw what happened and thankfully didn't say a word.

Grade seven was Mr. McIsaac and Brother O'Reagan. Mr. McIsaac was our main teacher, and Brother O'Reagan taught us social studies. Mr. McIsaac had a sense of humour at times. He was teaching us science one day and talking about food as nourishment. He said, "If you happened to cut yourself, you wouldn't see a carrot floating in your blood, but the nutrients from the carrot are there." We all thought that was pretty funny. He was an alcoholic, and after lunch we could smell alcohol on his breath. Once I am sure he passed out in class. His eyes were closed and we just sat there quietly until he woke up.

He could also be cruel. My friend Doreen reminded me about an incident that happened in Mr. McIsaac's class. None of us had been able to answer a math question that he had assigned us to complete by the end of the day on Friday, so he called us all back to class on Saturday. He said that if we didn't get the question by the end of Saturday afternoon, we would have to stay on into the evening and we would miss the Saturday night movie. He called on Doreen along with Louie Duncan to answer the question, but they stuttered so badly that they couldn't give him the answer. He said, "Look at the two smartest pupils in this class and they can't even answer a simple question! Take a good look, everyone, because they aren't so smart now, and they will make all of you miss the show!" He then sat them back to back in the middle of the room and ridiculed them. Doreen and Louie conferred back and forth until they came up with the answer but, because of their stuttering, they couldn't get it out. Finally, they gave Mr. McIsaac the answer on a piece of paper, and we were all able to go to the show. Doreen quit stuttering after she left the Mission.

Brother O'Reagan was even worse. We all knew not to mess around with him. I don't think I ever saw him smile. Brother O'Reagan taught us Greek history for part of grade seven. As miserable as he was, I did look forward to going to his class because Greek history fascinated me. Once while he was giving a lesson, Liz Sargent was cutting her fingernails with a clipper, and the noise could be heard throughout the classroom. This made Brother O'Reagan extremely angry, and he gave Liz the strap. I was very surprised to learn years later that Brother O'Reagan helped a few Native people get small bank loans. I couldn't imagine him doing a kind deed for anyone and, if he hadn't helped my mom get a two-hundred-dollar loan, I probably wouldn't have believed it. It just seemed that this was a different Brother O'Reagan than the one I knew at the Mission. He died of a brain tumour a few years after the school closed and before a few boys could charge him with sexual abuse.

I can visualize every classroom in the Mission school building except for the grade-four room. When I try to remember grade four, I draw a total blank. I don't know what the classroom looked like or who the teacher was. Nothing! It surprised me because I had so many memories of other times in my life, before and after grade four. I even remember what the grade-two classroom looked like, even though I didn't spend any time there. It was right across from the grade-three class. I asked my brother Mike if he remembered the grade-four teacher and he said, "Yeah, it was Mr. Kokee. He had a son named Roland in our class. They were Dutch and Mr. Kokee had lots of maps. He was a pretty good guy."

It is surprising how many students have forgotten years or extended periods spent at the Mission. A male friend of mine and a former student from the Mission did not remember an incident that had happened to him until he watched a docudrama about the Mount Cashel Orphanage that aired on CBC called *The Boys of St. Vincent*. He said that while he was watching the program, memories started hitting him like bricks. He remembered the sexual abuse he endured; he remembered who and where it happened. Some draw a total blank about almost their entire time at the school. Why I can't remember grade four is a mystery to me. Dolly suggested that maybe it was a really dull year and there was nothing special to remember. I hope she's right.

My brothers Bobby and Mike Sellars at St. Joseph's Mission, 1965

CHAPTER 4

I Get
Religion
But What
Did It Mean?

Before bedtime at the Mission, we would kneel in the centre aisle of the dorm and say our nightly prayers. We usually recited ten decades of the rosary, which took a long time to do. By the time we were into our third or fourth Hail Mary, our knees were pretty sore from kneeling on the hard floor. If the nun wasn't looking, we would sneak and sit back on our heels. We were told that was a sign of disrespect to God and, if we were caught sitting, we were punished by having to kneel longer or we were given the strap. It was always a treat when we could find little ways of making those nightly prayers a little less painful like when Anne (Michel) Stinson would say the prayers. She had kind of a lisp and sounded cute and sometimes even comical when she prayed. I enjoyed listening to her, which made the prayers go faster.

Sometimes for punishment, we had to kneel for long periods of time in the nun's room or in the doorway beside her room. If I was given a choice between getting the strap and kneeling as a punishment, I would pick the strap. The strap is over within a few minutes and the pain is not as prolonged as with kneeling. Rose Sellars and Anne Stinson had to kneel outside the nun's room until the next morning when they were caught throwing a ball back and forth while lying in bed. Anne said she had a hard time kneeling and staying awake. She and Rose and any of us did as we were told without question or we got harsher punishment. We always envied the priests and nuns kneeling in the chapel on benches that were padded with soft cushions. Even as an adult, I cringe when I see a baby crawling or someone kneeling because it makes my knees hurt to watch them. Throughout her life, it was painful for Gram to kneel. She always wondered whether our knees were so tender because of all the praying and kneeling we did. I wonder the same thing.

Gram was from the Carrier tribe, and Xp'e7e was Secwepemc. Both were fluent in their languages, but none of their kids or grandkids learned to speak either language. Part of it was because they were from different tribes, but the main reason was because of the Mission.

Not once in all the years I had lived with Gram did she speak one word of Carrier, and I assumed that she did not speak her language. I was so surprised to learn that when she was taken to the Mission she spoke only Carrier. I asked her why she didn't speak it now and she said angrily, "They whipped us when we spoke our language!" Once she and her sister, Annie, got to the Mission, Gram said they had to learn English quickly. Gram did not teach her children how to speak Carrier because she knew they would be attending the schools and she wanted to spare them the agony of being punished with the strap. Like so many Aboriginal parents who were fluent in their Native tongue, she did not pass on her language to her children. She spoke only English to them.

I was surprised that Gram and her sister did not speak the Carrier language to each other once they left the Mission. Years later when my grandmother was in her eighties, my friend Ellie, who was fluent in Carrier, came to our house. After all those years, Gram wanted to take the opportunity to speak Carrier with our visitor. But Ellie had gone to the Mission too and she had been taught to be ashamed of speaking her language. She would not speak Carrier with Gram and Gram was disappointed. When speaking the language always resulted in being strapped for it, I imagine it would be hard to now just start speaking it on cue.

The only word I use in Carrier is *Aloo*. About a year before Gram died, my daughter, Jacinda, was pregnant with my first grandchild. I became a grandmother at the age of forty-two, and I thought that the endearment "Granny" made me sound too old. I wanted something that reminded me of Gram and her traditions, so I asked her how to say "grandmother" in Carrier. Gram, who by this time was a hundred years old and had trouble hearing, replied, "Aloo." So I asked my grandkids to call me Aloo, and they still call me that today. Later, I found out that Aloo means mother and not grandmother. I guess Gram thought that I was asking her how to say "mother" in Carrier.

The kids at the Mission were not allowed to speak their Native languages, but the irony of the nuns speaking French to each other was not lost on some kids. Although we would never tell the nuns to their faces, many of us resented not being able to speak our language freely when the nuns openly spoke the language they had learned as children. Even though I did not learn how to speak either of my Native tongues, I did learn to speak Latin by following the Catholic mass.

We went to church on Sundays. The Catholic mass at that time was recited entirely in Latin. We had lessons every day to practise how to respond to the priests during mass. We practised until we got it right, with proper pronunciation of the Latin words and when to say them, but the meaning was not translated into English for us. We were, as usual, just little robots programmed to do everything on cue. We were not at residential school to get a well-rounded education.

During one part in the mass, we all had to bow our heads in prayer. I was always so curious about what the priest did while our heads were bowed. I wanted to look up and see what he did, but I was too terrified the nun or one of the tattletale girls would see me with my head up. I knew if they caught me, I would get the strap. I never did find out what the priest did during that part of mass. For all I know, he could have been dancing a jig.

The nuns were always eager to listen to the girls who wanted to tattletale on whoever looked sideways at the boys in church or who giggled, talked, or did anything wrong during worship. Despite the belief that church was something that was supposed to be so sacred, and that we had to be so respectful, we were encouraged to squeal on other kids who "misbehaved" in church. The nuns all sat right at the back of the sanctuary and often couldn't totally keep an eye on us. After church, the nuns would have a list of numbers collected from the squealers. I was on that list a few times. A few times, I was guilty because I would respond to someone who was talking to me in church, but a few times I wasn't guilty. Once you were on the list, there was no way to prove your innocence. All you could do was take your punishment. There was no appeal. If someone said you were guilty and the nun believed her, then you were guilty. Some girls got even with other girls by telling on one another.

There was one church holiday when we would have to go and pick wild rose petals and put them in a huge basket. We would all line up two by two behind the priests and nuns, except for two girls who would be ahead of everyone, and throw the rose petals onto the path where the priests would walk. This was repeated all the way to the statue of the Virgin Mary that was up by the graveyard. We walked there slowly, the priest said part of a prayer and we answered with the other part of the prayer, and then we knelt around the statue and had a ceremony. I have no idea what that was about.

Going to confession was equally comical. In fact, some of the comical things we did at the Mission were usually during times we should have been the most serious. Every week, we had to go and confess our sins to the priest and we had to tell him how many times we committed each particular sin. Often we would lie about the sins we committed that week. We made up sins because there was no way the priest would believe we hadn't sinned, and we probably would have been punished for lying if we said we were free of sin. We would go to confession and say, "I lied four times this week and I thought bad thoughts three times this week. I was mean twice this week." We would be given our penance and away we would go for another week. At the trial investigating sexual abuse charges against our principal, Father Hubert O'Connor, a woman from Sugar Cane testified that young girls who had no idea what adultery was nevertheless would confess to it. They heard adultery was a sin, so it seemed logical to confess to it. I'm sure none of us was ever sorry, but we went through the motions that were required. Things said in the confessional were not punishable by the strap. We were given prayers to say and everything was forgiven.

We still had to go to church on Sundays at Soda Creek when we went home for the holidays. The priest would come around our community of Deep Creek in his little Datsun pickup and cram as many Indians as he could in the back and drive us up to Soda Creek. The truck had a canopy on the back but it had no door so we were constantly breathing the fumes from the exhaust that would settle in under the canopy as we drove. My grandparents usually sat up front, squished in with the priest. Once we had arrived at Soda Creek, my cousin Phyllis and I would wait for her younger brother Art to go into the confessional; then we would run inside the church. Art, all of eight or nine years old, had such an imagination that he would tell the wildest tales to the priest and would recite his confession loud enough for everyone in church to hear. We had a hard time keeping our laughter in, and eventually we would have to run outside the church and have a good belly laugh. Art provided us with many entertaining moments, and we always looked forward to hearing his "confessions."

At Christmas, we put on a concert for the White people around the area. I'm not sure who they were, but they packed the playroom and we did a show for them every year. Our Aboriginal parents were not invited. During the concert, we had to talk as the Bible was written, and every year kids would be the brunt of jokes for their part in the play. I was ridiculed the year I had to say, "Go ye that way," while gesturing with my arm in a certain direction. I was a shepherd, and I had to direct the Wise Men towards the baby Jesus. Doreen (Paul) Johnson and Christine (Pop) Patsey teased me for months after Christmas. They thought it was such a big joke. I don't know if it was the way I said it or that it just sounded so funny.

One day in church, months after the concert, Doreen and Christine were still making fun of me and laughing. I was mad at them and refused to talk to them. Thank goodness, because someone squealed on them for giggling in church and they got the strap after church. It is the one time I felt a little satisfaction in someone getting the strap. I reminded Christine of this incident years later, and she started to laugh again. She remembered it and told me that once, in a Christmas play, she had to put on the head of a donkey and she couldn't see because the nuns had not made any eye holes in the costume. She stumbled around, and the nun got mad at her for being so slow. We laughed and laughed that day about some of the silly things that happened at the Mission.

For mass on Sundays, we dressed up in the uniforms that the nuns made – navy-blue tunics with white blouses underneath. We had to be very careful not to dirty them. The nuns took great pride in their creations. The uniforms weren't any great works of art and didn't require any more than basic sewing knowledge, but the nuns made sure that we knew how much time they had spent on them and we had better take care.

The nuns always picked on a girl from my community because she had a protruding stomach, and they would single her out in front of all the other children. You could tell this young girl, who was only about five years old, was deeply ashamed of her protruding stomach, but the nuns had no concern for her feelings. The nuns took pride in saying that they could sew any uniform, *even* one that would fit her. They said her protruding stomach was from malnutrition at home. I don't know what caused it, but other children in the same family did not have protruding stomachs, so I'm pretty sure it wasn't malnutrition. The girl's family had a huge garden every year, and everyone in our community always had a good supply of wild meat. If this girl was suffering from malnutrition, it was malnutrition from the residential school and not from home. The nuns, in their wisdom, even though they had never been to the home of this girl, had an answer for everything. They didn't take her to see a doctor to find out if there was anything that could be done to correct the problem.

Because the nuns ridiculed this girl, it encouraged ridicule from other kids. Kids can be mean at the best of times but, when you are in a situation where negativity surrounds you 95 percent of the time, kids can be downright cruel to satisfy their own negative feelings. We really had to be careful we didn't violate anyone's turf or offend someone by appearing better than anyone else, like what happened when someone would get new shoes. If our shoes got too small for us, the nuns would usually give us hand-me-downs from older girls. Only when the hand-me-downs were so worn that no other girls could wear them would the nuns break out a new pair. This should have been a joyous occasion, but *no one* wanted to get the new shoes. With new shoes came the burden of trying not to *look* at your new shoes. The other kids saw this as "showing off," and that could easily earn you a punch or two from someone. Other kids, especially our rivals, watched like a hawk to see if we were showing off with our new shoes. If word got around that we were too proud, we became the target of more kids. We quickly learned to keep our heads up so our eyes didn't look at our shoes. We *never* mentioned our new shoes and hoped they would be broken in quickly so that life could carry on without us having to worry about looking at them.

The message of "don't try to be better than anyone else" had an effect on me for years. The more invisible I was, the better. The more mediocre I was, the better. *Don't strive to be the best, strive to be the least!* And it was seen as okay to be the least.

We had a saying at the Mission if we did anything stupid. We excused ourselves with the line, "Oh well, I'm just an Indian." Mom remembers being called "Dirty Indians," "Stupid," and other derogatory names by the authorities at the Mission. I don't remember being called names, but we got the same message. What a messed-up world in which to raise an impressionable child. What a messed-up world in which to raise whole Nations of impressionable Aboriginal children.

I got a lot of agony at the Mission because of my fair skin. I was a "half-breed," and it showed. I suffered more than a few abusive remarks and knocks, but I didn't think anyone but me remembered how I was picked on because of my light skin. But Eileen Peters remembered. Eileen was one of the kids who stayed year-round at the Mission. She and her siblings had no home to go to; their mother was dead, and their dad was a wanderer. One summer, they stayed with my aunt Annie, and they could have stayed at other places too. I can't imagine how that affected them, and years later I was so thankful for having a solid home to go to during the summer and Christmas holidays.

I had never been close friends with Eileen, but we always got along, even after we left the Mission. Years later, when I heard that she had lost her arm in a car accident, my youngest son, Tony, and I went to the hospital in Williams Lake to see if we could cheer her up. I felt bad for Eileen because she never really had a chance to have a good life. I went to the hospital thinking that Eileen would be pretty depressed. When I got there, Eileen was really glad to see me. We started talking about the accident and she said, "You know, Bev, it could have been worse. I could have lost more than my arm." She had such an upbeat attitude that she seemed to be consoling me for feeling bad for her. As is often the case with people who went to residential school together, our conversation got around to the Mission. She said, "I remember, Bev, that you always got such a rough time for your fair skin. I didn't like how some kids picked on you, but

I couldn't do anything about it then. If it were today, though, boy, they would have to answer to me."

Cecilia LaCeese was another one who had fair skin and suffered for it. Anything "different" was cause for some sort of attack. Kids needed to put down other kids because they didn't feel good about themselves. It really was a breeding ground for dysfunction. The nuns and priests were not there to make sure everyone's rights were honoured. They were there simply to herd the kids around and make sure they collected their "per capita" for each Aboriginal head. There were no attempts to mediate between kids or teach any social skills.

We were also there to work and earn money for the school. When my grandmother went to the Mission, she said they hardly did any schoolwork and did hard labour most of the time. The children did everything from planting and harvesting the gardens, to cutting wood and keeping the fires going in the heaters, cutting and hauling in the hay, looking after the livestock, and anything else that required manual labour. My mom remembers going to school for half a day and then working the rest of the day. In 1951, the half-day labour program at the schools officially ended and children started to go to school for the full day but were still required to do a lot of labour before and after school.

By the time I attended, chores were less of a money-maker for the school and more part of day-to-day maintenance of the school. During my years at the Mission, I worked in various parts of the building. I was assigned to the priests' dining room and later to the nuns' dining room doing their dishes and making sure the table was set for the next meal. We washed their floors, polished their beautiful dishes and silver, and made sure their fancy drinking glasses were spot free. When we worked in the nuns' dining room, they took inventory of every piece of food they had not eaten and then checked to see that it was loaded on the serving tray before it was sent back to the kitchen. I liked working in the priests' dining room because they did not do an inventory of any food left over and there was a bit of time after they left and before the nuns came in to check on us, so we could quickly gobble down a piece of toast or something.

Another reason I liked working in the priests' dining room was that they read the local newspaper and would sometimes leave it on their dining table. We would quickly scan through it to see if there was any news about any Native people we knew. It was one of these times that a cousin of mine found out that a man from Soda Creek had died. He had frozen to death in Williams Lake. Of course, there was nothing we could do about it. We didn't go home for funerals. We usually didn't hear of things that happened in our communities until we went home. The priests went out every Sunday to our communities, but they didn't give us any news about our families.

I also worked in the chapel on the main floor and in an adjoining room where the priests kept their robes for mass. The nuns assigned only girls they thought deserved the honour and, in their eyes, I qualified as a good girl – scared stiff to do anything wrong is more accurate. When mass was over we had to clean the chapel and altar, clean the candle holders, wash the goblet that the priest used to drink wine during mass, and hang up his robe. We were warned not to touch the wine and bread hosts that were in the little room off from the chapel because God would punish us if we violated his trust. One girl who worked with me in the chapel would eat some of the hosts that we were given during the service. I felt so guilty. I was sure I was the one who would go to hell because I didn't squeal on her. I was more scared of what the girl would do to me if I squealed on her, and thought I would deal with God's anger towards me when Judgment Day came.

Another one of my duties was to work in the kids' dining room, washing tables and dishes and mopping and waxing the floors. Before each meal, the older girls who were the servers went down and got food from the kitchen. Each table had twelve children. When the servers had the table prepared, we entered the dining room two by two and stood at our place at the table. When all the boys and girls were in their place, we said prayers. From there, the two servers dished out the food. We ate in silence. There was always a supervisor, a priest, brother or nun, in the dining room. Sometimes they would read from the Bible while we were eating, and sometimes they would just walk back and forth down the aisles. Later on when we started to get lay supervisors during meals, we were allowed to talk freely among ourselves. After meals, the two older children at the head table would stay behind and do the dishes for their tables, and all the rest of the kids would go and do their assigned chores.

Once at home when Mike, Bobby, and I finished our meal and then piled our dishes in the middle of the table and the cutlery neatly beside it, Gram got visibly upset. I was surprised because her voice cracked when she said, "You kids don't have to do that! Just leave your plates where you are sitting." It was rare that I saw Gram get emotional, but that day I think it distressed her to see us so conditioned by a place she hated.

Each weekday was the same at the Mission. Chores were done before we went to class, and our outings were confined to the schoolyard and to the girls' side. Saturdays were the big clean-up days. This was the day for everything to be done thoroughly. The floors were not just washed, they were waxed and shined. The silverware in the dining rooms was polished, the dorms were cleaned, and the windows washed. Clean clothes were delivered from the laundry in a big bin that was rolled into the dorms.

Sunday afternoons were special, though, because we went for walks if the weather permitted. We lined up two by two and walked on the road, or we went to Yellow Lake, which was a couple of miles from the building. Once in a while, for a really special treat, we were allowed to build a fire, and the kitchen staff would deliver, in lieu of lunch, enough buns and wieners for us to have two hot dogs each. Other times we would go across the road above the school and into the hills, where we were allowed to spread out. We all had "houses" that we constructed with tree branches or a piece of old plywood we

Cariboo Indian Girls' Pipe Band outside St. Joseph's Mission. The door with the big cross at the front of the school building is where Father O'Connor (the principal) and other priests and brothers would stand and watch the kids. My sister Jean was part of the pipe band and is somewhere in this picture. My sister Dolly was also part of the band but she is not shown. Photo postcard circa 1965. Photographer Ken Buchanan. Published by Lakeside Colour Productions Ltd, Williams Lake. Courtesy Rein Stamm found for roofs. In our house, we made mud cups or, if we found old glass or the discarded lid to a tin can, we would put it in our house and use it as a piece of cutlery or something. Some even found old broken cups, and they had "nice houses." We had tea parties and invited other kids to come and share in our hospitality by offering them some cactus (we ate the inside), *alec* (kinnikinnick berries), *seg wouh* (rosehips), white berries, wild onions, chewing pitch (spruce gum), or whatever else we had found that we knew we could eat. We didn't have tea, but imagination was a good substitute. Each time we returned, we had a bit of housekeeping to do because the wind would blow down our walls or the rain would carry away parts of our houses. One girl ran away and hid there until she was found. She didn't want to be at the Mission, but she didn't know how to get back to her family, and I guess our playhouses were as close as she could get to being home.

After our Sunday walks we would go back to the school, and the older girls would go to benediction, which was Sunday-afternoon mass. No one ever offered an explanation why the junior girls were let off this duty. I was just glad that we didn't have to go. We had enough praying without going to church twice on Sundays.

CHAPTER 5

The Body Was No Temple

When we went on our Sunday walks in the spring and fall, we often stopped to fill our empty bellies with edible plants and berries. We had grown up on the land and had gone out with our grandmothers to pick berries and with our grandfathers to hunt. As a result, we knew we could chew on wild rhubarb, wild celery, and onions, or stuff kinnikinnick berries into our mouths. We knew the land could sustain us and supply everything we needed to survive. But the nuns didn't respect our knowledge and thought we would poison ourselves. So we ate only when the nuns were not looking.

We felt hungry all the time. I can remember my stomach aching and feeling empty. Many times, though, I could not eat the food at the Mission. One member of my community once said, "The way they treated us, they must have thought of us as animals ... you don't treat human beings like that. The food they gave us you wouldn't give your dog!" I agree with him. I learned to wrap what I could not eat in napkins and then throw it in the garbage so that it looked like I was just throwing away paper. My cousin June (Sellars) Porter, who worked in the Mission kitchen in the early 1960s, was asked to serve rotten macaroni to the children; she refused and almost got fired from her job because of it. She and other workers dumped the rotten food in the pig container before they were forced to serve it.

Once when I was doing chores in the dining room, I witnessed a young girl, Junie Paul, get caught throwing food into the garbage.

Junie had made the mistake of scraping her food directly off the plate into the garbage can. A nun saw her and made her dig the food out of the garbage and eat it. Of course, the food was now mixed with other garbage. Junie sat there crying and gagging, trying to get the food down. If she had vomited, she probably would have had to eat that too.

During another period, the food got so bad we just couldn't eat any of it. Instead of throwing out the rotten morning mush, the cook, who had a heavy Dutch accent, mixed it with the soup at lunch. We couldn't eat that, so the mushy soup was mixed with the supper. This went on for a couple of days before the mess got so bad it just had to be thrown out. There were many hungry bellies in those days.

There were the rare exceptions to the rule. Every now and again, a dozen girls and a dozen boys would be chosen for a special meal. I know it was a dozen because that is how many could be seated at one of our dining-room tables. On special occasions like being "Confirmed" or "Making Your First Communion," a few children were allowed to celebrate with special food.

I was seven or eight years old when I was chosen to make my First Communion. Along with the other catechumens, I wore what I can describe only as a miniature white wedding dress with a veil. When I was confirmed a few years later, I wore the same kind of white dress and veil, but this time I also had to pick the name of a saint for my confirmation name. I picked the name "Yvonne" because that was the name of my sister Dolly's best friend. Her nickname was "Peanuts," and she was almost as special to me as Dolly. I picked the name because I wanted a little something of hers to be close to me. We were eventually assigned the name of a saint if we did not pick one. I didn't know if there was a saint named Yvonne and was pretty happy to find out there was. So my official Catholic name became "Beverly Ann Yvonne Sellars." I still don't understand the significance of having another name. I didn't question it then and I don't care to understand it now. All I cared about was having Yvonne's name.

The highlight of First Communion and of Confirmation was that after the ceremony we got that special meal and were the envy of the other kids. In the weeks before, we talked about this moment among ourselves and couldn't wait for the time to come. During the ceremonies, all I could think of was the celebration breakfast that was waiting for me. I was so careful to make sure I didn't do anything wrong so I could get my reward. Finally, we were led into the dining room where two tables, one on the boys' side and one on the girls' side, were each set with a white tablecloth and a vase of flowers. And there was the breakfast we were waiting for: *corn flakes, toast, an orange, and juice!* As kids who were fed garbage all year, we savoured that simple meal like it was a breakfast fit for kings and queens. To this day, I am not sure nor do I care what the significance of either ceremony was, but I remember thoroughly enjoying that special breakfast.

The food at the Mission was just as rotten when my mom went there and she especially remembers the oatmeal mush that was cooked the night before and became hard by morning. To top it off, the milk they were given was sour, and there was no sugar to sweeten the dish.

My grandmother and her generation were probably fed the worst food because there were no refrigeration services back then. My grandmother remembers being locked in an attic for two weeks because she wouldn't eat the rotten meat she and other students were served. She and a girl from Canim Lake were punished because they wouldn't eat it. Gram says the girl from Canim Lake lasted a week and then agreed to do her penance and eat the food. Gram stayed in the attic for two weeks before she gave in. For two weeks, another girl was made to bring Gram a bit of bread and some water each day. "Just because we were Indians they thought we could stand anything," Gram told me.

Even at age ninety-six, Gram still remembered what they were fed at the Mission because they got the same meal day after day. At every breakfast during the nine years she spent there, they got a piece

·of bread dipped in tallow and mush with no sugar or milk. The tallow was dry and cold by the time they got it, and the mush was hard. For lunch, they got broth with bits of toast floating around. The kids never got toast for breakfast but, if there was some left over from the nuns and priests, they got it for lunch in their broth. She also remembers some kind of big green leaves in the soup. For supper they got meat, which was rotten a lot of the time, boiled together with potatoes. Gram says that once they got a roasted potato. They weren't served butter or salt with it but, still, it was a real treat for them.

The only time they got a change in diet was at Easter. They got one very soft-boiled egg with the white part of the egg very runny. Gram thinks they just dipped the egg in hot water. At Christmas, they were given boiled blood to drink as a "treat." Mom remembers having baked blood for a Christmas treat. I asked Gram if she liked the boiled blood, and she said, "We had to like it. We were always starving." At the same time she remembers mouth-watering smells coming from the sisters' dining room, where the nuns and priests had their Christmas fruitcake, pudding, and the works. The nuns also had a small Christmas tree in their private dining room, and a couple of times they invited the children in to see it. Of course, the children did not have a tree of their own.

Heroes come in many forms, and for the kids at the Mission in 1966, our hero was Pat Joyce. That was the year Pat was hired as head cook. Before he arrived, the kids were served different meals than the nuns, priests, and staff. As in my grandmother's and mother's time, we would have to watch carts of good food roll by into their private dining room. It's easy for the authorities at the school to say the food was good because they never had to eat what the children did.

Pat refused to follow the separate meal policy. He insisted that we be served the same good food as the priests, nuns, and staff. Pat told me years later that he couldn't believe the garbage they were feeding us when he first arrived at the school. After Pat came to the

Mission, we all looked forward to mealtimes. We even asked for second servings. Sometimes there would be food left over in the big cooking pots after all the tables were served. Pat and his staff would leave it on the counter by the kitchen, and the kids who served at each table could go and get a bit more for their table. This did not sit well with the nuns, and they started to preach to us that "gluttony is a sin." It was as if they couldn't stand the thought of us enjoying something. I did not make the connection until years later, but one of the nuns was obese. Someone should have told *her* that gluttony was a sin!

Children from the residential schools have all kinds of stories about stealing food for themselves or their siblings. Even though the schools raised cattle and had vegetable gardens, the children did not receive this good food. Most of us just endured the conditions. Some girls made raids on the kitchen and sometimes I heard the boys raided the cellar where vegetables were kept. But I was never part of that – I was too scared to get the strap.

Quite often during my time at the Mission, I suffered from what the nurse said was "yellow jaundice." My grandmother says she came down with yellow jaundice a few times as well. I was sent to bed and would vomit until it seemed my guts were going to come out. I remember thinking my vomit always smelled like raw fish that had sat out in the sun too long. Years later, my grandson Orden was handling raw chicken while helping his mom cook dinner. He ended up with food poisoning because he did not wash his hands properly afterwards. In his symptoms and from the smell of his vomit, I recognized the "yellow jaundice" Gram and I suffered on a regular basis. Gram says there was no medication to cure "yellow jaundice" in her time. I wasn't given any medication that I can remember either.

In fact, there were no doctors at the school. There was a nun we called "the nurse," but she didn't work with a doctor. She was the only one who looked at us when we were sick. My sister Dolly broke her leg while out on a walk when she was about eight years old. The nuns and the rest of the group left her behind. But two older girls, Ida Duncan and another girl, had been lagging behind and heard her crying. Ida carried Dolly back to the Mission, where Dolly stayed in bed until she could walk again. She received no medical treatment and no cast. Dolly remembers the nuns praying by her bed because they thought God would heal her leg. Ida and the other girl were not rewarded for their good deed. Instead, they got the strap because they were late getting back.

Another time, a group of girls were out for a walk and my cousin Phyllis fell out of a tree. She was crying and in a lot of pain and couldn't get up. We were about a mile away from the Mission, and the nun told another girl and me to help her back to the dormitory. We carried her back and put her to bed. She didn't go to the hospital. She just stayed in bed until she was mobile again. I don't remember how long she spent in bed, but it was a few days.

If children got too sick in my time at the Mission, they were sent more than two hundred miles away to the Coqualeetza Hospital in Sardis. In my mother's and grandmother's time, though, sick kids were sent home to die. When my mom went there, she remembers a girl, Katherine Timothy, who broke her leg and was sent to bed. She was in bed for a long time with no medical treatment. Eventually, her leg became infected and gangrene set in. Mom said that the whole dormitory smelled of the gangrene. The girl was sent home to the Chilcotin and soon died.

My uncle Ernie was one of the kids sent home. Gram said the school sent him home because he had tuberculosis and they didn't expect him to live. He was so happy to be home that he would try to jump and run around. But he had no strength at all, and his legs would buckle under him. Gram's sister, Annie, had learned all the Aboriginal medicines from their mom and, like her, felt she should try to help the people who were suffering. Annie showed Gram different types of plant medicines, and Gram tried them all. Slowly, Ernie got better.

He never did go back to the Mission once he was well. Ernie didn't
know how to read and write, but he could mentally calculate numbers
faster than we could on paper. He loved to show us up in that area.

I was hospitalized once while I was at the Mission. I had been goofing
around in the playroom with a group of girls and tried to climb onto
someone's shoulders so she could pack me around. It was a dumb
game, but everyone was always trying to prove who was the "toughest." I fell off and onto the concrete floor, landing flat on my back. I
immediately felt intense pain and couldn't move. The nun came over
and told a couple of girls to help me up and take me to the dormitory.
I couldn't make my legs work, so the girls had to grab me under my
arms and pack me up three flights of stairs. They put me to bed and
I was left alone in pain.

Eventually, I needed to go to the bathroom. I knew I had to
get to the toilet, because I would get the strap if I wet the bed, but
no one was around to help me. I managed to ease myself out of bed
and onto the floor. I started to crawl and pull myself along the two
hundred feet to the washroom – past the junior girls' dorm, almost to
the intermediate girls' dorm. The washroom was on the other side. I
made it only to the divider between the junior and intermediate girls'
dorms. I lay on the floor in excruciating pain and began to cry. Nearby
was the huge iron door that led to the stairs. From the stairwell, the
maintenance man, Bill O'Donovan, heard me crying and came in to
see what was happening. I told him I needed to go to the bathroom.
Would he help me? He said he would be right back and returned
with the principal. Father O'Connor called an ambulance, and I was
taken to the hospital in Williams Lake.

When I got to the hospital, they put a tent over my lower body
because even the weight of the sheets was too heavy for my legs. I
don't remember how long I was there. It couldn't have been more
than a week. But I was glad to be in hospital because the priests who
lived at the Mission regularly visited our community, and I thought

for sure they would tell Gram and Xp'e7e what had happened to me. Every day, I anxiously waited for my grandparents to come during visiting hours. Every time someone appeared at the door to my room, I expected to see my grandparents. But they did not come. When I was finally well enough to return to the Mission, my heart felt heavy on the way back.

It was still painful for me to walk; I could barely climb the stairs to the dorm. I was also in trouble with the nuns because Father O'Connor had found out about my accident. They were so mad at me they wouldn't lighten my workload, and I still had to do all my chores and whatever the rest of the kids were doing. My cousin Phyllis and other friends would help me when the nuns were not looking. It took a long time before I was able to walk without pain.

When I went home for the summer holidays, I asked Gram why they had not come to visit me in the hospital. She was shocked to hear that I had spent time there. No one had told them about my injury. Poor Gram, she worried about me and my sore back after that. Even when I grew up and I would complain about backaches, she wondered if I had suffered permanent damage from that accident.

Years later, Bill O'Donovan came to court and stood by the former students when Father O'Connor, by this time appointed bishop, was charged and convicted with multiple counts of sexual assault. If it were not for Bill O'Donovan, I would not have gone to hospital and would have stayed in the dormitory without medical treatment until I could walk again. As far as I know, I am the only student who was taken by ambulance to the hospital during the years I spent at the Mission.

The dentist usually came out to the Mission but once I had to go into town to get my teeth fixed. I was horrified when I saw it was Mr. Calhoun who would be driving me. Mr. Calhoun was an ex-military man brought to St. Joseph's Mission to discipline the kids – a common tactic used in many residential schools. He was a tall and well-built man. Although the girls did not have too much to do with him, he would not hesitate to discipline a girl if he saw her doing something "wrong." He was the boys' supervisor. Bobby and Mike had stories of beatings Mr. Calhoun would give the kids. My brother Morris remembers a time when Mr. Calhoun made him kneel in the boys' playroom on the concrete floor. It was five hours before Mr. Calhoun returned to release him, and Morris was in extreme agony. Mr. Calhoun just laughed and told him, "Oh, I forgot about you."

Kids warned others to stay clear of Mr. Calhoun or, if we encountered him, to do exactly as he said. When I saw Mr. Calhoun standing at the car waiting to drive me to the dentist, I shuddered and climbed into the back seat of the car. All the way to Williams Lake, I tried to keep as quiet as I could. I did not want to get him angry.

Mr. Calhoun dropped me off at the dentist's office and, when he came back, I was sitting in the waiting room in a lot of pain because of the dental work. I got up immediately to get my coat. To my surprise, Mr. Calhoun reached above me and took my coat off the rack. He then helped me put it on. He also put his hand on my shoulder as if to comfort me. That little act of kindness has stayed with me all these years. Maybe it was just so out of character for him or maybe at that moment I really needed and appreciated some comfort. Who knows why I remember? After that, I was not so scared of Mr. Calhoun, even though we did not say a word to each other on the way back to the Mission or have any other encounters that I can recall.

In a world where compassion was almost non-existent, we remembered even the smallest bit of kindness. One priest from Williams Lake said that the kids mobbed him when he visited the school. What did he expect from emotionally starved children? Mr. Calhoun's name was never mentioned when former students started naming people for abuse at the school. I now feel Mr. Calhoun should have been charged for the beatings he gave to the children, but people were too focused on the sexual abuse to bring charges for any other form of abuse.

Mother Germaine was the head nun at the Mission. She was quiet, older, slim, and of average height. She had an office and bedroom on the main floor. She didn't have much to do with the kids; she didn't supervise them and she didn't teach. Instead, she had mostly administrative duties. In all my time at the Mission, I had only one encounter with her and it involved Sister Loretta, who was not popular with the kids. They called her "Tomato Face" because, when she got mad (which was most of the time), her face would turn beet red. I was glad I didn't get her as a teacher but, for a short while when I was about ten or eleven years old, I was assigned to work with her in the schoolhouse. Then, for some reason, I was transferred to work in the main building. As usual, I didn't ask any questions; I just did as I was told. A few days after I was transferred, I was leaving the main floor and had passed by Mother Germaine's office. I was about to go through the big iron door to the stairway when I ran smack into Sister Loretta. She grabbed me with her sharp fingernails and threw me against the wall. She had me by my shirt and was holding it up against my neck. Her face was two inches from mine. I'm sure my feet must have been touching the floor but, at the time, the sensation was that she had lifted me into the air. Sister Loretta demanded to know who I had spoken to in order to be transferred from working for her. The thought never occurred to me that I *could* talk to anyone about getting other work. I tried telling Sister Loretta that I had spoken to no one, but she would not believe me. She was really upset, and I could feel her anger in the death grip she had on me. From her beet-red face and short breath, I got the impression that she really wanted to harm me.

She was almost out of control when Mother Germaine stepped out of her office. In a firm, cool, and controlled voice, Mother Germaine said, "Sister Loretta! Can I talk to you, please?" Sister Loretta let me go and I scooted back to my dorm. After that, I was nervous every time I saw Sister Loretta coming, fully expecting that she would finish what she had started, but she never did. Mother Germaine must have told her to leave me be. Thank goodness for the few people who would not allow the children to be treated badly.

Visitors who came during the school year were shown to a parlour beside the principal's office. The kids were called into the room for a visit supervised by a priest or a nun. Gram and Xp'e7e came to visit once in the five years I was there. I was so excited when the nuns came and told me my grandparents were there. Mike, Bobby, and I were all taken to the parlour. Gram and Xp'e7e were sitting on one side of the room and we were made to sit on the other. A priest sat between us to "supervise" our visit. We couldn't be free with our grandparents the way we were at home. We were scared to do or say something wrong with a school authority sitting there, so we all sat quietly in our chairs. The priest did most of the talking. Gram and Xp'e7e didn't stay long. They probably felt the strain of the visit too. They had gotten a ride over to the Mission with someone from Soda Creek, who was supposed to pick them up later. They didn't wait and started to walk home. It broke my heart to watch them leave as I stood at the dormitory window.

The small pleasures that we could have had were always tainted with some negative imposition on the part of the church officials. Visits were censored, and so were letters. While I was at the Mission we saw on TV images of the war in Vietnam. I didn't know anything about the war except that men over there were sick and wounded and they needed help. It was beyond my comprehension how people could kill each other like that. I desperately wanted to do something for them. I thought of writing to the president of the United States and offering my services in the hospitals. It did not occur to me at the time that they would never accept the services of a little girl. I thought about writing many times, but I knew it would not get past the nun. So I ended up doing nothing because I was also scared that the nuns would ridicule me.

The priests and nuns screened all our mail. One girl from Canim Lake, Margaret, had to rewrite her letter home three or four times before the nuns agreed to send it. Once a year Gram would send us five dollars to be divided among her grandchildren. I thought it strange that there was no letter with the money. I asked Gram when I got home and she said she wrote a letter too. I'm sure Gram didn't enclose an escape plan or anything drastic. The goal was to discourage any contact with our home communities.

The nuns even went so far as to write letters for children. While I was doing research in the national archives in Ottawa, I found three letters supposedly written by my grandmother, her sister, Annie, and another girl from Soda Creek. They were all glowing letters home about how happy they were at the school and how good the sisters were to them. Gram was really upset when she saw the letters. She barked, "I hated that place from the minute I got there until the time I left." All the letters were in the same handwriting and said pretty much the same things. Gram read the letter signed by Sarah Baptiste (her maiden name) and noticed the words she would not have used. It said, "Dear Father," Gram says she would have written, "Dear Papa"; that's what they called their dad, not "father." "Father" to her was a priest. I didn't get a chance to ask my auntie Annie before she died if she knew anything about the letters, but Gram says Auntie wouldn't have written that letter. She hated the place as much as Gram did. It's interesting to note that these letters ended up in the archives. Why weren't they ever sent home if they were meant for Gram and Auntie's dad? I suspect because of an investigation that might have been happening, someone other than the children wrote them just to make it look like the kids were happy.

There were not many visitors while I was at the Mission. I always found this strange because I knew the parents missed their children. Later when I grew up I found out that at one time in some areas "Indians" needed a pass from the Indian agent to leave the reserve. If they didn't have a pass they were put in jail. The pass was put into place to prevent militants from gathering, to prevent potlatches and other events, and to prevent Aboriginal parents from visiting their children in off-reserve residential schools. Even though the pass system was not enforced after the 1950s, I assume the lack of visitors at the school was partly a hangover from those days.

Grade six, Cariboo Indian School (St. Joseph's Mission), 1965–66. This is the only picture of me at the Mission that I can find. I am to the extreme right, sitting down in the second row

From left, back row: William Sandy, Reg Michel, James Lulua, Marvin Jeff, Willie Alec

Third row: Shirley Sampson, Doreen Johnson, Maureen Boyd, Susan David, Adam Jimmy, Chris Amut, Louie Duncan, Jerry Quilt, Irvine Harry, Antoine Phillips

Second row: Margaret Dick, Marcella Dixon, Arlene Archie, Margaret Daniels, Rose Sellars, Liz Sargent, Dorothy Johnny, Alice Abbey, Bev Sellars

Front row: Danny Archie, Lyle John Archie, Ernest Archie, Michael Sellars, Eric Sargent

CARIBOU
INDIAN SCHOOL
GR. 6
1965-66
LAKESIDE STUDIOS

CHAPTER 6

A Few
Good
Memories

Contrary to what some people might think, I do have some good memories of the Mission. I made some lifelong friends, and even the kids who I did not get along with when we were together at the Mission became my friends once we left. We seemed to sense that we shared a common bond of understanding and pain and we allowed ourselves to talk about it with each other. Most who went to the schools did not speak of their experience to others who had not shared it. I spoke to my grandmother and mom about the schools but, until our experience there became public knowledge, I did not tell my kids about it. They knew I went there but that was all. I think that was common for most students who went to the schools.

When the conversation turns to our time at residential school, sometimes we reminisce about the fun we found together because, surprisingly, the weekends could be enjoyable. After we did the big clean-up on Saturday mornings, we had lunch and we were able to play outside, where we hung around in little gangs. Our yard had eight swings and one slide, but they weren't as easily accessible as one would think. Whoever got to the swings first would save the other swings for their friends, and sometimes fights broke out for control of the swings. Sometimes they were given up when we knew someone was going to get candy.

Saturday afternoons were canteen days, and those who had money were allowed to buy sweets at the canteen. We were not allowed to have money on our person. The nuns kept track in a book of how much money each kid had, and there was a limit on how much we could spend. Kids with money were popular and most grudges against them were dropped for a short time.

Gum was something that everyone enjoyed having, but it was not sold in the canteen. The only gum we had access to at the Mission was "spruce gum" that we peeled from the bark of a spruce tree when we went for a walk. That left a bitter taste in the mouth. Older girls who went into town for high school sometimes would have store-bought gum. During my first two years at the Mission, my older sister Dolly was employed at the school and, on her paydays, she would come and ask what I wanted from town. My answer was always the same, "Gum." When she asked what kind, I usually picked among Juicy Fruit, Doublemint, or Spearmint. I thought it was expensive but, once, to be brave, I thought I would ask for all three. She didn't blink an eye and brought back three packs of gum just for me. Other kids knew Dolly bought me gum, so I was popular for a while when she would come back from town.

Fresh gum! If someone was chewing gum and they were a friend, we would ask them if we could chew the gum after them. Usually, someone might say, "No, Rose is chewing it and then Penny and then you can chew it." The gum usually went around to quite a few kids and, if you were in line to chew the gum, you made sure you got it when it was your turn. The gum always had an "owner" and if the owner wanted the gum back then you had to give it whether everyone had their turn or not. It was a big deal to be "in" on chewing someone's gum. I laugh now and think how many germs must have spread that way. The older girls who went to school in town told us that the White kids thought chewing old gum was disgusting, but to us it was just making do with what we had. Store-bought chewing gum was something that could be shared, and so we did. It was no more disgusting than the food we were forced to eat.

With time to kill on Saturday afternoons, the girls played records and danced with each other in the playroom. My cousin Edie (Sellars) Woods always tried to get her younger sister Phyllis and me to dance but, by this time, I had already learned to be painfully shy. I wanted so badly to get up and allow my body to move to the music, but my mind told me not to do it. I was always so guarded against being ridiculed and, even though I love to dance, I never did dance at the Mission. Once in a while the older girls and boys were allowed to have dances. They would gather on the boys' side of the building in the playroom, and under heavy supervision they would be able to mix and dance with each other. I was always too young, but we got lots of reports from the older girls about all the flirting that went on.

Saturday night was movie night. If we were not being punished, we could go. First, though, we had to have our hair curled so we were ready for Sunday morning mass. Some had curlers put in their hair; others secured their curls with bobby pins. I liked to make ringlets by braiding or twirling my hair around strips of rags because it was easier to sleep with them than with the curlers or bobby pins that poked the scalp and made sleeping very uncomfortable. With kerchiefs on our heads and curlers in our hair, we would all head over to the playroom on the boys' side of the building where the movie was shown. The boys were usually watching *Hockey Night in Canada* on TV when we arrived at the playroom. The Montreal Canadiens and the Toronto Maple Leafs were the teams they cheered for, and there was a friendly rivalry between people who cheered for opposite teams. Most of the girls weren't hockey fans, and we waited patiently for the TV to be turned off so the movie could start. We would sit on the left side of the playroom and the boys would sit on the right. On each side of the room the juniors sat in front on the floor, the intermediates in the middle, and the seniors in the back. The older girls would make eye contact with their boyfriends, and a whole lot of flirting and giggling went on behind us younger ones.

It was funny to watch the way the older boys and girls interacted with each other on movie nights. They also had ways of connecting at other times. The nuns would not let the older girls get too close to the older boys, so they had to find other ways of flirting with each other. The doors into the playrooms were at opposite ends of the dining room and, if a girl left the dining room first, just before she went out the door to the playroom, she would look back at her boyfriend. He would be standing on the boys' side of the dining room watching her. There would be eye contact and a giggle from the girl and an ear-to-ear grin from the guy. This would continue until the dining room was empty. If a girl liked a guy and she turned around and the guy wasn't looking, that was a rejection. Or, if a guy was watching and the girl he liked went into the playroom without turning around, that was also a rejection. This was the best way to keep track of who the couples were.

Couples couldn't hang out together, so the older girls would hang around with their boyfriend's sisters or cousins. If the sister of their boyfriend was younger, they would look out for her. That lasted until the couple broke up, and then they moved on to the relatives of their new boyfriends. My first boyfriend at the Mission was Danny Archie from Canim Lake. We never got anywhere near each other and just exchanged glances from across the room. I was told through the grapevine that he liked me, and I let it be known that I liked him too, so we became boyfriend and girlfriend. We lost touch when we left the Mission and Danny became one of the many statistics for Aboriginal people. He committed suicide at a very young age.

Every once in a while, a couple managed to sneak out and be together for a brief time. Liz Sargent was one of those and gave us a detailed description of the kiss she and her boyfriend managed to sneak behind the school building. She told us she almost passed out because their kiss lasted so long and she could hardly breathe. The conclusion I came to after hearing about her experience was that kissing could be life threatening.

There were rare times when the girls and boys were allowed to mix without any real restrictions. One of these times was skating in the winter. All the girls' skates were kept in big cardboard boxes under the stairway, and we would have to hunt through the boxes to find two skates of the same size. Sometimes we ended up with two different sizes. They were old and the blades were dull, but they served their purpose.

The outdoor ice rink was on the boys' side of the building. The rink was lit up with floodlights, and the skating rink boards were piled high with the snow the boys had shovelled. The first time I was on skates I managed to walk to the outdoor rink, but then I just pulled myself along the boards. Mike saw me and, as the ever-protective, older brother, took responsibility for teaching me how to skate. He pulled me along until Bobby showed up to take over. Mike would go skate and then come back and relieve Bobby. It wasn't long before I was skating on my own.

My brothers Bobby and Mike played hockey. I heard Bobby was a good player, but I never saw either one play hockey. The school bus from the Mission would take them to town when they had a game against non-Native teams. My cousin Lenny was said to have moves as good as Gordie Howe and could have made something of his talent if he had the right coach. He and other senior boys were fast and dangerous skaters because they would play tag with each other and in the process knock down those who could not get out of their way quickly enough. Edo Chelsea once knocked me over so hard I couldn't breathe. He was playing tag, skating fast, trying to get away from being tagged, and he knocked me down. But he grabbed me under the arms, still skating and laughing, and stood me up. Eventually, I was going as fast as he was and I guess he thought I could stop by myself so he let me go when someone else tried to tag him. I kept on skating fast but couldn't stop and hit the boards hard. Wham! Despite the bruises, I loved being on the ice. I was free to be with my brothers, even if it was just for an hour or so. I have a distinct memory of standing by the rink

Brother Robbie (left) and some of the boys who played hockey, circa 1965

Back row, from left: Gilbert Johnson, Brian Bob, Jerry Charleyboy, James Lulua, Floyd Daniels (in jean jacket)

Front row, from left: William Sandy, Billy Peters, Lenny Sellars (my cousin Lenny was smaller than the others boys because he was younger and should have been in PeeWee League. They moved him up to Bantam because he was so good) boards watching all the kids skating. It was dark but the floodlights were on and everyone was having a great time. I stood there looking at the kids on the ice and then looked up at the stars and it felt magical.

Something else we did to entertain ourselves was to ride inside tractor tires. We could fit two and sometimes three kids right inside the rims of a big tractor tire. We took turns riding the tire or guiding the tire while someone else rode. We would push our coats inside to cushion our heads, back, and bum, and then down the hill we went, with four or five other kids running behind to make sure the tire didn't go where it wasn't supposed to go and to slow it down when it got onto level ground. We used two sizes of tires. One was a smaller tire from the front wheel of a tractor. It was a snug fit for one child, and most of the kids preferred the bigger tire, which could fit two or three kids. We would cross our arms and hold on to the rim, then put one of our legs on the chest of the kid across from us to make sure no one fell out of the tire.

We had only a few tires to play with and there was always a battle between the boys and girls to keep the tires in the play area on their side of the building. If we girls had a tire on our side, one of the older girls would watch at mealtime to make sure none of the boys left the dining hall. If they left a little too early, we knew they were out to steal our tire, and the older girls would sneak outside to prevent it from being stolen by the boys. If they had it, we snuck onto their side of the building to look for it. When the nuns asked how we got the tire, the girls would tell them the boys accidentally rolled it onto our side of the building and we wouldn't give it back.

There were times when the big tire picked up too much speed and got away from us and the kids inside had a pretty rough ride. Once, just as the tire was going down the hill, the whistle blew and we had to go inside the building. The girls running with the tire let it go and ran into the building. After a very rough ride, the girls inside got out to find no one around. Although we had a few bumps once in a while, I don't remember anyone getting seriously hurt riding in tires. I later found out that my sister Jean had started the riding-in-tires craze at the Mission. It made my heart swell a little that my sister was the originator of something that had lasting positive memories for many of us.

When we were out on the playground, or anywhere for that matter, whenever we heard the Secwepemc word St7leck, that was our warning that someone of authority was coming. Kids moved like lightning when they heard that word. It's good for a laugh today when we remember some of the things we got away with. It's even funny now to think of some of the things we didn't get away with, although it sure wasn't funny at the time. I guess the sense of humour that Native people have is just another way of survival for us.

In our community, Rick and David Pop were great for turning tragic situations into humorous ones when something tragic would happen or we would be talking about something that was painful, often it was hard to deal with. At these times, Rick or David would get a mischievous look and would say something to make it funny. The other would pick up on it, and they would begin to feed off each other. Pretty soon we would be howling with laughter. We joked about our lives and the things that happened to us, otherwise we would have drowned in our tears. I was so grateful for their crazy humour many times.

We had a TV in the basement playroom, and we would huddle around it. Some sat on the floor, some sat on wooden benches, and some stood behind everyone else. Sometimes about a hundred of us would be trying to watch TV at the same time. I was so impressed that Doreen (Paul) Johnson knew the names of the TV programs. Doreen and her family had a TV at home in Lac La Hache. Later, I was equally impressed with a schoolmate in the eighth grade who knew how to use a telephone. I was eight years old in November 1963 when we saw on TV that President John F. Kennedy had been shot. The nuns got so upset and the assassination bothered me as well. The images of violence I saw on television were almost too much to comprehend, and I could not imagine how people could live in that world.

The media and its messages had devastating effects on me in other ways as well. On Saturday movie nights at the Mission, a cartoon or short film would be shown before the main movie. In *Black Arrow* (1944), the Indian was always the hero, with Black Arrow, son of a Navajo chief, getting justice, retribution, and revenge by the end of each of fifteen short episodes. It seems strange that the priests and nuns would allow even one of those segments to be shown to us, because the storyline ran contrary to all their other teachings about Aboriginal people. We were never the heroes.

Another one of the short films that ran before the movie was more in keeping with the general philosophy at the Mission. In *Beautiful British Columbia* (1940), all of the people on camera were White, and they were inviting other people to British Columbia to witness the beauty of it. I couldn't have been more than eight years old, and I couldn't form the right questions then, but, basically, I found myself thinking, "Where do we fit in this society?" I couldn't understand why there was no mention of Indian people, and I put as much thought into it as an eight-year-old could. The words "invisible" and "undesirable" in this context hadn't yet made it into my vocabulary.

Most of the movies we watched on Saturday nights at the Mission reinforced the myth that being Indian was something to be ashamed of. One movie, it could have been *The Silent Enemy* (1930), showed an elderly Indian woman who had been thrown out of her teepee because she was too old to help with the family. The rest of the tribe did not want her around anymore. One scene showed her fighting with the dogs for scraps of food that were tossed her way. At the time, I couldn't differentiate between fact and fiction. Even though I knew that did not happen in my community, I believed somewhere in my "Indian" world we were that cruel and I felt such shame.

One Saturday, we were all excited because we were told that we were going to be shown an Elvis Presley movie. A lot of the girls were crazy about Elvis. The show was a western, but I don't remember the name of it; maybe it was *King Creole* (1958) or *Flaming Star* (1960). We were all enjoying the movie until I heard Elvis say something like, "I'd rather kiss a dog than an Indian." It was like he reached out of the screen and slapped me. I can't remember the context of his remark, but that one line has stuck with me all these years. As an adult, I mentioned this to Violet Stump and she said, "I remember that." We were absolutely feeling ashamed about ourselves as "Indians" and this celebrity, who a lot of people were absolutely crazy about, confirmed to the world that Indians were not even as good as dogs. What a terrible thing for vulnerable, young Aboriginal children to hear. Years later I heard that Elvis was part "Indian." Whether it is true or not is irrelevant now but, if we had heard at the Mission that Elvis was part Indian, the message would have instilled in us such pride. Instead, we heard him shame us.

There were plenty of derogatory remarks about Indians in western movies, and we saw many westerns. Of course, at the time, I could not see it for what it really was: stupidity on behalf of racist fools right down the line from the producers who created the films to the administrators who chose them for our "entertainment." Instead, I cringed and the shame I felt at being Indian went deeper and deeper each time I heard a derogatory comment about Indians. The flip side to that, of course, was the "perfect" White families shown on TV. They were perfectly manicured, their homes were immaculate. Everything about them seemed perfect and, because I did not know any White families, I assumed this to be the truth for all White people.

Living near a redneck town where people made no bones about how they felt about Indians did not help matters. People in the area called in to a radio program called *Open Mic* to talk about things they felt were important. Many times I would cringe when they started openly talking about "the Indians" and the "Indian Problem." People would be so cruel in their comments about Indians. Those comments always made me physically and emotionally ill. It was at those times that the shell I used to protect myself came up and I retreated deeper inside myself.

Messages I was getting from everyone around me at the Mission told me that I was inferior to White people. Messages I got from my family were telling me the same thing. My grandmother had gone to the school for nine years where she was brainwashed into believing she was inferior to White people, and she relayed that message to me in different ways. Some of my uncles and brothers who had gone to the school relayed that message to me. White society relayed that message to me in their words on the radio, in the actions in their everyday lives, and in their TV shows and movies. The schools and other agencies that were created to look after the Indians also relayed that message. Everything in society told me that I was not good enough because I was an Indian.

CHAPTER 7

Pain, Bullying, But Also Pleasure

In addition to the daily ritual of kids getting the strap for wetting the bed, hardly a day went by without someone getting the strap for another reason. Kids were strapped in a place and at a time when all the other kids could see, and it was a battle between the kids, the nuns, and the priests to see which kid would break first. Kids tried not to cry when they got the strap or at least not to cry until they had received a few whacks. If you cried on the first whack, the other kids ridiculed you for being weak. The longer you could hold out without crying, the tougher you were seen to be. Some kids did not cry at all when they got the strap. I really envied them. One of the first times I was in line to get the strap, one of the other kids told me not to cry. But the pain was like taking a knife and slicing your hands and arms. I was always ashamed if I cried too soon. Some of the reasons I remember getting the strap were for getting a ball that fell on the other side of the fence, talking in church, being too close to the boys' side of the playground, not moving fast enough for the nuns, and being late.

It got so we were scared to do anything at all. They really did control us by fear. That feeling lasted into my adult years. Even though I knew I wasn't going to get the strap once I left the Mission, the fear of being punished for the smallest things took years of hard work to overcome. Once I was strapped on the legs for wearing a dress without wearing jeans underneath. We were required to wear dresses for meals but with jeans underneath so that our bare legs didn't show. We did wear dresses without the jeans to church and to class, so I didn't see any difference in wearing just the dress to dinner. We were in line waiting to go to the dining room when I was yanked out of line. The nun started strapping my bare legs and accusing me of wanting to show them off to the boys. That was the furthest thing from the truth. If it occurred to me that the boys would look at me because of my bare legs, I would have tried to wear two pairs of pants. When I went to bed that night I could still see the strap marks on my legs. I was no more than seven or eight years old and still learning not to do *anything* unless I was told.

When I and my brothers Mike and Bobby were in grade three, Bobby came to class one day with huge welts on his arms. He also had welts on his back and could not lean back against the chair. I don't know who gave him the strap, because no one ever asked why kids got the strap. I felt so bad for Bobby, but there was nothing anyone could do about it. Even if he got the strap because one of the authorities was in a bad mood that day, then that was the way it was. To whom would we complain? Our parents and grandparents could do nothing. Bobby would have been the ripe old age of nine when he got that beating. There was no reason in the world why someone so young should have been tortured like that. There is no reason why anyone, no matter how old, should have gotten that kind of treatment. People defending the churches try to justify giving the kids the strap because it was common in those days for school and parents to use corporal punishment. I am sure the kids in public school did not go home beaten black and blue from the strap. I am sure kids in public school were not beaten with the strap on a daily basis for the least little thing. I am sure kids in public school were not strapped until their spirits were broken. I doubt if any of those students bear scars from the strap today. You can bet that their parents would be right at the school to complain about the brutality of it.

We didn't have anything except the priest's or nun's conscience to protect us, and many times their conscience went out the window. Because children would struggle to endure the strapping for as long as possible without crying, the authority figure would strap harder or somewhere the skin was more tender and that would hurt more. The older ones who attended the school during my sister Dolly's time said there was a nun who they swore had an orgasm when she would strap kids. They said her face got all red and you could tell she really enjoyed giving the strap. I have to wonder how much of the priests' and nuns' personal frustrations were taken out on the children.

Some of the staff did try to stop the extreme abuse. One day, we were eating supper and the dining room was quiet except for Brother Sprite, our supervisor for the meal, walking around reading aloud from the Bible. The dining room door came crashing open and all heads turned to see what was happening. The boys' supervisor, Cyril Aucoin, came marching down the aisle of the dining room from the boys' side with the strap in his hand. Brother Sprite was standing in the centre of the dining room in the aisle that separated the boys' side of the dining room from the girls' side. Cyril marched over to him, fuming. Cyril held the strap to Brother Sprite's face and said, "If I ever hear of you using the strap on one of those boys again, *I'm going to shove it up your ass!*" Brother Sprite's face turned beet red, and you could tell he was frightened of Cyril Aucoin. I'm sure I wasn't the only one silently cheering, "Yay! Way to go, Mr. Aucoin." We didn't dare make a peep right then, and just continued to eat our food silently, but Cyril Aucoin was a real hero to me that day. Father O'Connor ended up firing Cyril.

Because of the number of beatings I received from the strap as a child, I am surprised at how programmed I still am to endure pain. An incident that happened after I was an adult illustrates this point. I once slipped and fell because of water on the floor of the local supermarket and severely sprained my hand, especially my right ring finger. I eventually had to go for physiotherapy. During treatment, the physiotherapist put small electrode points on both sides of my finger to stimulate the muscles. He asked if the strength of electric current was okay. I had not had this treatment before, and did not know what to expect, so I said yes. The physiotherapist left to attend to another patient and said he would be back in a few minutes. It turned out that the stimulator was set too high and the points it touched on my skin started to burn. I could smell my skin burning, and yet I did nothing. I did not scream out or even move. When the physiotherapist came back, he saw what was happening and quickly took the electric rods off my finger. "Didn't that hurt?" he asked. I felt stupid because I should have known to take it off, but programming from residential school would not allow me to go against a White authority figure. I still have small scars on my finger where the burn marks are. Over the years I have endured other pains without question that "normal" people would not tolerate.

With all the abuse inflicted on us, it is no surprise that we often turned on each other with bullying and taunts. In order to avoid the bullying at the Mission, you either had to have a protector or you had to be part of a "gang." For the first few years while I was a junior girl, my protector was Doreen (Paul) Johnson. I don't remember how our friendship started, but I was extremely thankful it existed. Girls thought twice about messing with me because they would have to answer to Doreen. One older girl was jealous of my friendship with Doreen. On a weekend that Doreen was away, the girl cornered me in the playroom. She grabbed me, threw me up against the lockers, and slapped me around a few times. This girl was about five years older and a whole lot tougher. She warned me not to breathe a word of the incident to Doreen or else I would really get it. When Doreen got back I immediately told her what happened, and Doreen went and smacked that other girl around. She never bothered me again, and once we had left the Mission, I eventually became friends with her.

When I moved up to the intermediate girls' dorm while still a junior, I joined the gang of Nancy Archie and Lorna (Boyce) Amut from Canim Lake and June Boucher from the Quesnel Band. Our "gang colours" were black, and we tried to be first to get black shirts out of the laundry bin when it came to the dorm. We protected each other and became great friends. Nancy and I kept in touch on an irregular basis until she died in 2001 of complications from chronic alcoholism.

Fights at the Mission were common. The biggest one I ever saw started with my cousin and another Secwepemc girl. They got along most of the time, but something came between them, a fight started, and, pretty soon, girls from the two communities were fighting. It was a knock-'em-down, drag-'em-out brawl. My cousin Phyllis and I stood and watched her older sister Bernice come storming into the playroom from the dorm upstairs. She looked as mad as a wild woman, jumped right into the fight, and took out a few of the rival girls. Phyllis and I were quite impressed.

I was moved up to the intermediate girls' dorm partway through grade seven and ended up being the only junior girl there. Even though I was only eleven years old, I went to study hall with girls older than me and, by the time I got back to the dorm, all the younger girls would be in bed. The advantage of being moved was that the intermediate girls did not have a nun for a supervisor. They had two young women from Vancouver, Miss Donna and Miss Helen. Miss Helen told us stories about going to school from home and doing her homework in her own room. I liked listening to her stories. It was like reading a book. She took you to a place far away where good things happened.

Shortly after I was moved to the intermediate dorm and before I joined the gang of Nancy, Lorna, and June, I had gotten into a fight with one of the other intermediate girls. Not only did I lose, but the other girl's friends turned on me, and I found myself being tormented by many. I was sitting on my bed in the intermediate dorm licking my wounds. Miss Helen came in and sat beside me. She put her arm around my shoulder and asked, "What's the matter?" I tensed up and would not tell her. She let her arm drop. The rules of the game said that if I told, not only would things have gotten worse for me but also I would have been branded a crybaby. I rode it out with my tormentors until things settled down.

The way my body reacted when Miss Helen touched me needs some explanation. While I was growing up with my family at Deep Creek not once did they hug me or tell me they loved me. I did not miss it, nor did I ever question their love for me. They expressed it by the things they did for me. When we knew we were not going to see each other for a long time, we did not hug or even touch. We just said goodbye and left. If we felt sad we did not show it. If we got physically hurt, we were fixed up and told to be careful. That was the way it was. When I was about fifteen years old I went to the airport with Mom and Lawrence, and saw Buster and Millie Hamilton there putting their daughter, Nina, on the airplane to Vancouver. Millie was kissing and hugging Nina. I thought they were the weirdest people I'd ever seen. I had never seen such emotion openly expressed. Only in the last years of her life did Gram begin to write in cards that she loved me. She tried to tell me she loved me a few times, but it was awkward for her to say it and awkward for me to hear it. I was glad when she went back to just putting it in a card. I raised my kids the same. I cuddled them when they were very young but, even though my love never lessened, I stopped the physical contact as they got older. My daughter, after spending a year in Portugal as an exchange student, was the one who started to hug me. I was so uncomfortable at first, and I'm sure I stiffened up when she hugged me, but over the years it has become easier to hug others or to accept hugs from others.

Each of the generations of women in my family learned during their time at residential school not to touch and that there was no touching except when you were being abused in one way or another. It does not take long to brainwash a child, and those of us who spent years at the school soon learned to fear physical contact. When

Miss Helen was trying to comfort me, I did not understand that she was touching me in a compassionate, acceptable way.

Some of us learned to fear human touch for other reasons. Some of us were chosen to be in the girls' pipe band or on the baseball team, and the boys were in hockey or air cadets. Father O'Connor and the other priests would stand at the main entrance to the school and watch the kids as they played in the yard. They didn't have to; the nuns were there, but they did anyway.

I was chosen to play drums in the pipe band. Linda, a senior girl, came to me in the playroom and told me I had to start taking drum lessons after school. I wasn't asked or given a choice. I did as I was told and, on certain days after school, another girl and I went to a room on the second floor where we took lessons from Linda, who was already in the pipe and drum band. I enjoyed our time together, and I enjoyed playing the drums, although I wished I could have been picked to play baseball instead. I envied the girls who got to play baseball, but there was nothing I could do about it so I settled into playing the drums.

I was all excited when I heard that the pipe band was going to Expo 67 in Montreal. St. Joseph's Mission was known for its band, with its bagpipes and bass drums and girls in kilts and sporrans. Both my older sisters had played in the band, Dolly on drums and Jean on bagpipes, although Dolly had left the Mission by the time I started. Even though I was one of the youngest in the band I knew I could play the drums as well as any of the girls who had been in the band for a few years, and it did not even occur to me that I might not go to Montreal.

One day after practice, Cyril Aucoin said he wanted to talk to me. Cyril was one of the band instructors as well as the boys' supervisor. He and Brother Robbie were the favourites of the kids. There were certain people the kids were not afraid of and Cyril was one of them. Cyril said, "Let's go for a walk; I want to talk to you." On our walk, he told me that I wouldn't be going to Expo. He said that the band was going to have to walk about five miles in the Expo parade, and they didn't think I was strong enough to carry the drum that far. He assured me there would be other trips. I wanted to cry but of course I didn't. I wonder now if I could have carried that drum for all those miles. At the time, I was sure that my determination would have given me the strength if they had only given me the chance.

Years later I realized I had dodged a bullet, because Father O'Connor sexually assaulted some of the girls during the Expo 67 trip. All his victims seemed to be in the band at one time or another. I wonder whether he personally picked the girls for the band while standing at the main entrance of the building and whether I might have been one of his future victims.

It's not that I got away untouched, though. It was when my chore assignment was to clean the dining room that Brother Gerard would follow me around. I would only have been eleven or twelve years old at the time. Brother Gerard would stand too close to me, poke me in the ribs, rub the back of his hand against my body, and say things that made me shudder. I stood frozen in fear and dread whenever I saw him coming. He was an authority figure, so of course I couldn't say anything to make him stop. I was never so relieved when, shortly after he started to hang around me, I heard Brother Gerard was gone. I know he had definite plans for me, and it still scares me because what could I have done about it if he had decided to take me somewhere and take advantage of me?

Who could I have told? The nuns? They were in the dining room supervising us while Brother Gerard harassed me. They could have said something to him – but didn't. I don't think they were dumb enough not to know what was going on. Could I have told the principal? I didn't know it at the time, but he was sexually assaulting a number of girls. Could I have told my grandparents when I got home? What could they have done? I guess like so many of the children at residential school, I would have been repeatedly abused with no way to stop it. If we complained about something, nothing was done about it; if anything, it made matters worse.

When certain priests were later charged with sexual abuse, Brother Gerard's name came up with a few girls, but formal charges were never laid against him. Father O'Connor, later Bishop O'Connor, was the only principal ever charged and convicted. Four principals in a row should have been charged, three of whom became bishops. If the top people at these institutions were abusing, it is easy to see why the others were allowed to abuse so freely. These days I have a hard time looking at anyone in a black robe without thinking that they probably are a sexual abuser.

As a child, I had regular nightmares about the cartoon characters Mutt and Jeff that made me wonder if my experience was similar to a TV show where a girl had nightmares about a clown. She later learned that she had a clown lamp beside her bed when her father sexually abused her. She had nightmares about the lamp and not her father. I wondered whether Mutt and Jeff represented an incident of that sort. Maybe I just did not like the cartoon show or maybe something had happened that was blocked from my memory. I also had a fear of lighted red exit signs. I remember those exit signs from Sardis because, when I got to the Mission, I lay in bed and saw them in the dorm. I remember thinking, "Oh no, they have them here too." I don't know why I thought that. Whenever I would see one I got a feeling I did not like and those strong feelings stayed with me until I was well into my twenties. I've wondered why those two things made me so uncomfortable.

After I left home at the age of five, it would have been very easy for anyone to abuse me without anyone doing anything about it. I was around adults who saw to my basic physical needs because it was their job, nothing more. I know I was physically and mentally abused, and what Brother Gerard did to me *was* sexual abuse. In addition, his coming into the dining room on a regular basis while I was working there would be considered stalking.

Some sexual activity was consensual, taking place between consenting adults. There were rumours about one nun being a bit too friendly with one of the brothers. Also, the nun who supervised the senior girls was caught in bed with one of the women who worked at the Mission. Another time, the same nun was caught in a broom closet with the same woman. Violet Stump and another girl were going in to get some brooms to do their chores. They opened the door and the nun and her partner were in very intimate positions. The nun got angry at Violet and told her, "You're supposed to knock before you come in!" Violet, now an adult, laughs, "Yeah, that's what you do before going into a broom closet. You knock!" It is strange to find out things about these nuns and priests who portrayed themselves as such saints.

I guess I could have run away to escape the abuse. Some kids tried. My brother PeeWee remembers when Ray ran away. Ray was about fourteen years old at the time, and PeeWee was two years younger. PeeWee was supposed to go with Ray and another boy. The three of them had been planning to escape the Mission for months. When they went for walks they secretly made bows and arrows so they would have grouse or rabbit to eat in case they had to spend time in the bush. Whenever they worked in the gardens they stole a potato. They collected what they needed for their time in the bush, put them in their stolen gunnysacks, and hid them where they could easily pick them up when they made their break. Finally, they were prepared to run. The plan was to go during movie night because everyone, including the supervisors, would be preoccupied with the movie and the room would be dark. PeeWee was watching the movie, when he looked around and realized that Ray and the two other boys were gone. He managed to sneak out of the playroom and ran out into the yard. He found his little bag and went into the field. He tried to holler for Ray, but did not want to holler too loudly in case someone from the building heard him. Ray and the others were gone and PeeWee did not want to try to run by himself. He eventually went back to the building, but the movie was over. Now he had to sneak into the dormitory. He managed to do so before the priests did their nightly bed checks. PeeWee was devastated and couldn't sleep that night. He thought of the boys in the bush and wondered if they would be caught. He felt like Ray was going to die that night. He also felt like he wanted to die because his big brother was gone and the loneliness overwhelmed him. He doesn't know what he did with his little bag that they had worked for months to put together. "Maybe it is still by that field," he says. I was shocked to hear Ray had left PeeWee behind. PeeWee said, "Maybe I was too interested in the show. I didn't realize when they left and then they probably couldn't wait for me."

Even something as simple as where to sit at the movies was not a decision we made. There was always some sort of order, and the nuns or priests placed you where they wanted you to sit. When they were ready to leave, Ray might not have been able to get PeeWee's attention without raising suspicion. I would bet that Ray waited outside for PeeWee until he felt he had to leave, and I would bet that Ray was in as much agony at leaving his younger brother as PeeWee was at being left. Ray went home, where Gram sheltered him and the other boy. Gram was usually completely honest, but I remember her telling an outright lie when the Royal Canadian Mounted Police or maybe the priest – I can't remember which – came looking. When we heard their car on the road, Gram told me, "Don't you say anything about your brother upstairs. You be quiet!" She didn't get up when the men came in but just kept sitting at the kitchen table and told them Ray was not there. After not being able to catch Ray for a few months, the authorities gave up. Gram was relieved that she and Xp'e7e were not thrown in jail for harbouring their fugitive grandson, but she said she just couldn't make herself turn Ray over to the priests.

I never tried to run away mostly because I was scared of the dark. I had heard stories of students getting separated from each other and having to spend the night in the forest alone. That thought just scared the dickens out of me because I would not have known which way to go to reach home. Most kids got caught on the highway or in town, and I knew I would have to go across back country to avoid the same fate. There were other reasons I didn't run, but I sure thought about it and talked about it with other kids. One boy was teased relentlessly because he said he was going to run away to Canada.

Sometimes there was a buzz about girls ready to run, but usually it was a well-kept secret. Some made it home but were quickly caught and brought back. The punishment for running away was severe. Some girls had their heads shaved, and the boys had to wear dresses. Of course, there was the ritual strapping in front of the other students to teach *us* a lesson. The message was loud and clear that this is what would happen to us if we ever tried to run away.

My cousin Phyllis was still a junior and probably about ten years old when she and some other girls attempted to run away. They made it just outside the boundaries of the schoolyard and hid in some big aluminum pipes used for creeks and culvert crossings. Their plan was to wait until dark and then head for home, but that's as far as they made it before getting caught and being brought back to the school. While they were waiting for it to get dark, they grew hungry and the only thing to eat in the pipe was tar. When Phyllis got back to the Mission, kids gave her a bad time about eating tar. They would say before we went in for supper, "Phyllis, you want some tar? I got some tar if you want that for supper." Then they would laugh at her. I felt sorry for Phyllis. I could tell she hated the teasing. Phyllis paid dearly for her part in the escape attempt. Thankfully, she didn't have her head shaved, but she got the strap and wasn't allowed to go to Saturday movie night for a few weeks.

Lucy (Jimmie) Alexis, Mable Laurant, and Geneva (James) Irwin, kids from a northern community about a hundred and fifty miles away, ran away but were caught and brought back to the school. Their heads were shaved and they had to kneel in the dining room between the aisles that separated the girls and boys so everyone could see their shaven heads. They then got the strap from Father O'Connor. Usually, that is where the story ends. The kids and authorities got back to their routines until someone else ran away. But for Lucy, Mabel, and Geneva, however, the story went a bit further. Once their punishment was finished, the girls were sent to the dorm. As they passed through the huge iron doors, they turned around and engaged the bolts to lock them. The priests and nuns couldn't get in. I don't know what their plan was, but we kids were all rooting for the girls. It made us feel good to watch the priests and nuns scrambling to restore their authority. In the end, the authorities got their way. Geneva told me later, "When we decided to let the nuns back into the dorm, we were locked in the underground tunnel that ran between the girls' side of the main building and the power plant where our heat came from. In the tunnel, we were left in pitch-blackness. Lucy put up a good fight and she still has scars from that incident. She had a couple of her fingers broken from the strapping she got. The only first aid she received was tying a popsicle stick to her fingers. She still has crooked fingers." Lucy, Mabel, and Geneva did not come back to the school the next year. I am sure the priests wanted to eliminate their influence on other kids. Geneva told me that Mabel died in 2009 and her only son hung himself in 2010.

My brother Bobby died when he was eighteen years old. They found him in a creek at the bottom of a cliff a month after he disappeared. We don't know whether his fall was intentional or accidental. During his preteen years, Bobby's personality changed drastically. He became very mean and was physically abusive. As a result, the relationship between us was hostile throughout our teen years. We even argued the night he disappeared.

One summer, when Bobby was eleven or twelve years old, Bobby and a young cousin of ours, Art, who would have been around eight years old, decided they were not going back to school in September. They hid in a cabin at the top of the ski hill just a few miles from our house. We all knew they were up there, but no one would say anything when the priest came to pick up the rest of us. The boys lived on a bag of puffed wheat they found in the cabin and wild berries around the cabin, and so earned the nickname my uncles gave them, "The Puffed Wheat Bandits."

Bobby and Art were up there a few days before the authorities finally found out where they were. The Royal Canadian Mounted Police and their dogs chased them over the mountain and across country all the way to Sugar Cane, about ten miles away. An elder at Sugar Cane hid them under his bed and sat on the mattress while the RCMP and the dogs searched his house. Bobby later ridiculed the RCMP by saying that the dogs were in the house sniffing around but did not detect him and Art in their hiding place.

They were finally caught and brought back to the Mission. I was in the girls' playroom when the RCMP came in with Bobby and Art. From the basement window we could see whoever walked by. There were two police officers, with the boys walking in front. The RCMP officer walking behind Bobby was holding his shirt at the shoulder and making Bobby walk a little faster. I remember the way Bobby's head hung as he was walking towards the boys' side of the building. I felt really bad for him at the time, and now I realize that look was one of a broken spirit. There was nothing he could do to end the sexual abuse, and I have to wonder if, like many others at the school, he was being abused by more than one person.

Bobby was a very angry young man, and his immediate family members felt his anger the most. I didn't question his anger at the time or try to understand him, because I knew nothing about emotions except to keep them hidden. It wasn't until the early 1990s, when our tribal council was doing a study into the impact of the residential schools that I found out my brother Bobby had been sexually abused at the Mission. Everything made sense then. I realized that, because he didn't know how to vent his anger, humiliation, fear, and whatever other emotions he was feeling towards the real cause, he took out his rage on the easiest target, which usually happened to be me. I have no doubt that had Bobby lived, his life would not have been productive or happy. The demons that tortured him were very visible when he died. I did not know while he was alive, but the sexual abuse, the physical abuse, and the emotional abuse he endured at the Mission were already taking their toll on him. Now I see so many of our people in the communities or on the streets, and I know the "help" they received to get where they are.

CHAPTER 8

Home
Sweet
Home

To this day, few experiences equal the joy I felt when we were finally allowed to take our "home clothes" down from the attic at St. Joseph's Mission. My home clothes represented the freedom I would soon have because of the holidays – two weeks over Christmas and two months in the summer. I joined in with the other kids comparing our home clothes, even though most of the clothes were not new. I was proud of the dresses Gram had made for me. Gram was a very good seamstress and sewed all of my clothes. The nuns never failed to inspect and comment on them. Maybe they found it astonishing that an "Indian" could sew that well. Sometimes my clothes were the envy of other girls too and one year a girl tried to bully me into trading dresses with her. I held my ground and went home with the dress Gram had made me.

After shedding our uniforms and dressing in more-comfortable home clothes, the next big excitement was waiting to be picked up to go home. Although the priests went into the communities and gathered up the kids when it was time to go back to the Mission, they never made any arrangements to send us home. That was the sole responsibility of our parents or grandparents. Some kids had to wait a day or so before their relatives came to get them. I would have been in agony if that happened to us, but Gram and Xp'e7e always made sure we came home the first day we were allowed to leave. It must have been a heartbreaking time for those who knew they would be staying at the Mission over the holidays.

On the day we were allowed to go home, kids stood at the window watching the long road that ran up out of the valley and into town. At the first sign of dust clouds or a flash of sunlight off of a shiny fender or mirror, kids would holler, "Someone's coming! Someone's coming!" We would all go dashing to the window and wait to see who was going home. It probably took less than five minutes for the vehicle to get down the hill and pull up in front of the school, but the wait seemed an eternity. Some kids knew immediately that it was their turn to go home because their parents owned vehicles, and the kids would recognize the car when it got close. My grandparents did not have a car but instead would hire someone to come and pick us up. Gram and Xp'e7e never came with the people they hired, so my brothers and sister Jean and I had to wait until someone asked for us.

During the Christmas holidays, most of the kids went home for two weeks. To make a bit of money during that short time at home, my brothers Mike and Bobby would snare squirrels and rabbits to sell. I enjoyed just being home and sledding on discarded pieces of plywood that we dragged back to the house. Bobby and Mike would heat them over our wood barrel stove and shape them into useable sleds. Unlike at the Mission, no one ever got mad at us for tracking in snow and melting it all over the floor. The water slipped between the cracks in the wood floor anyway. Home had such a relaxed atmosphere.

Just before Christmas, Gram and Xp'e7e would go to town and get the only turkey we had all year. Gram would splurge and buy one box of Japanese oranges. As well, she always ordered a package of Christmas candy and nuts from the Simpsons-Sears catalogue and she would pick it up while they were in town. Gram and Xp'e7e would come home on the bus, and we would meet them to bring the goodies home, dragging our homemade sleds up the trail from the highway to our house, a distance of about half a mile.

Every evening a few days before Christmas, Gram would start to ration out the oranges, candy, and nuts. After supper, Mike, Bobby, and I would sit around the table waiting for her to put out the treats. It wasn't much, a bowl no bigger than a normal soup bowl, but we would sit by the kerosene lamp and play cards or just talk about the things we did that day as we ate our sweets. Sometimes one of the adults would pick a few candies out of the bowl, but mostly they left them for us to enjoy. During the summer, Gram made a Christmas cake with the contents of a small bottle of rum she would buy. It was the only time she ever went to the liquor store, and my uncles teased her about it every year. She wrapped the cake in cheesecloth and stored it in a cool, dark place to let it age. By Christmas, we had a delicious dessert served with Gram's homemade jams on the side.

Everyone was home on Christmas Day. We didn't have a Christmas tree or presents. Gram, of course, did not allow drinking in the house, so having everyone together, a big dinner with a few treats, and the feeling of being secure inside a toasty warm house was hard to beat. We would also go visit other families in the community, get together with their kids, and go sledding. There were lots of things to do. Time at the Mission seemed to go by so slowly but, when we got home, our holidays went way too fast. We barely had enough time to get to know each other again before Christmas holidays were over and it was time to go back to residential school.

One year, it was minus-forty-five-degree weather on the day of our return journey. Mike, Bobby, and I wanted Gram to wait until it warmed up a bit before we tackled the cold walk up the path to the highway. She said we couldn't; the priest wanted us back by a certain day, and that's all there was to it, she said. By the time Gram had walked us up to the highway, we were all in pain from the cold. Gram waited with us until finally the Greyhound bus came. Mike, Bobby, and I got on, and Gram turned around to start back home. It made me so sad to watch her walking away by herself in the bitter cold. I knew she was already chilled to the bone, and I wanted her to be in a warm place like us. She told us when we returned home for the summer that she could hardly walk by the time she got to her sister Annie's place that day. Her sister sat her beside the warm wood stove, gave her a hot drink, and made her stay until she had warmed right through. Gram says she would have frozen to death if she hadn't had a place to stop and warm up.

Our return to the residential school after Christmas holidays meant another six months of chores, ridicule, and punishment before we could go to the attic for our home clothes and leave the Mission behind for two months of summer holidays. Our first days at home in the summer were always the same. My sister Jean would go out and get some *hooshum* (soapberries) – a bitter red berry that is whipped up until it becomes foamy and then is sweetened with sugar. Aboriginal people used *hooshum* as a treat but also for medicinal purposes to clean the blood and keep the digestive system regular. My uncles would laugh at Jean because the berries were not ripe when we got home at the beginning of our holidays in late June. Jean didn't care and each summer would whip up a huge batch of green "Indian ice cream." We all dug in, including our uncles.

My brothers Mike and Bobby would make bows and arrows right away. They made the bows out of juniper wood and the arrows from willow or cherry bushes. They cut, carved, sanded, and dried the wood. They made arrow tips from old tin tobacco cans or other scrap metal they managed to scrape together. They found feathers for the shaft and wrapped them on with sinews and glue. Once they had that all done, they would set matches to see who could shoot the straightest, the longest, or the highest. Gram and Xp'e7e did not allow them to shoot anything we could not eat, but Mike and Bobby had great fun hunting grouse and rabbits when asked to get some for supper. Everywhere they went, they also packed slingshots made from juniper wood and rubber from old tire tubes. Mike and Bobby did not like me using their big bows and arrows or their slingshots, so every year they would make me a small bow and some arrows. I was always so proud and thankful to my brothers for making me my own set. I never got my own slingshot, though.

Our summer holidays were full. We roamed the mountainsides looking for berries to eat. We played baseball with a sock wrapped around a rock and a two-by-four for a bat. We lay in the grass watching the clouds go by and discussed what object each cloud resembled. We were free – free to live life without constantly worrying about being punished. Free to roam the countryside without worrying about staying in boundaries. Free to talk to our brothers, sisters, parents, cousins, aunts, uncles, grandparents, and anyone we damn well felt like. Free to relish the feeling of security that having our family around us brings.

Of course, we had chores at home, but they were the minor chores expected of a child. We packed wood for the stove, we did the dishes, or we fed the chickens and pigs, but that was about all. Unlike at the Mission, we were not expected to do the majority of work. There were lots of fish in the creek that ran through our community and Gram sometimes sent us out to catch enough for supper. We would swim for an hour or two before we headed back with our fish. Some days we would be gone all day, but we were safe and could forage for wild celery or rhubarb, or more berries. We looked after each other and no kids were ever left to fend for themselves.

Some days in summer, if Xp'e7e was not using the horses, we would ride up and down the valley picking up other kids along the way. Xp'e7e had a number of horses over the years but, while I was growing up, we had Betty and Loco. Betty was a mean old bag and had the most uncomfortable trot and gallop. I hated riding her, and the feeling was mutual. Once she came charging after Bobby and me with her mouth wide open. Bobby and I surprised ourselves by jumping so high that we cleared the barbed wire fence with no problem trying to get away from her.

Loco, on the other hand, was the gentlest horse I ever knew. He would be lying in the yard, and I would go lie on his back. Later, with me still on his back, he would get up and start grazing around the yard. I had to hang on to his mane while he got up but, other than that, he did not try to throw me. The only time I ever remember being bucked off was when my cousin Phyllis and I were coming back from swimming. We were riding bareback crossing a field and had to jump a ditch. Loco landed on a beehive on the other side of the ditch and went wild. Although we were usually very good at riding bareback, this time Phyllis and I went flying off. My uncle Ernie sold Loco and Betty right after my grandfather died. Gram knew I would be upset and took me out for a walk to tell me. I was in mourning for Loco for years.

In the summer, Gram and Xp'e7e travelled by horse and wagon wherever we went. Mike and Bobby had a choice of whether they wanted to come too or stay at Deep Creek. I didn't have a choice. I went everywhere with my grandparents. Sometimes we went to Soda Creek or Williams Lake, and sometimes we went into the bush and camped. Xp'e7e hunted while Gram picked berries or fished in the lake.

Travelling on the paved highway allowed us to go quite fast. Whenever we spotted ripe berries, we would jump off, run over and eat some, and then try to catch up to the wagon to jump back on. If just Mike and Bobby jumped off, Xp'e7e would tease them by making the horses go faster, but the boys would run faster knowing Xp'e7e was doing it on purpose. They would eventually catch up and barely be able to pull themselves back onto the wagon, out of breath and laughing. I always wanted Xp'e7e to do that to me, but he never would. Xp'e7e would see me running, and he would stop the horses and wait for me to catch up.

Often on these highway trips, tourists would slow their vehicles to snap our picture. Gram hated being photographed, and I'm sure when the pictures were developed her scowl was evident. I wish I could find some of those pictures now.

During the summer, we also went into the fields with Xp'e7e and my uncles when they were cutting hay. Xp'e7e would bring in a load of hay on a sled made of logs that moved easily over the grass. Mike and Bobby would ride on the back of the load and slide off the hay as the sled moved along; they would then have to scramble to get back up the haystack. I wanted to do that too because they had so much fun, but Xp'e7e made me sit safely by his side. One of the things I did like about Xp'e7e favouring me was that I always got first choice of the horse I wanted to ride. If the boys were on Loco, I would simply tell Xp'e7e I wanted to ride Loco, and he would take Loco from them and give him to me. I was not popular with the boys when I did that, but I usually did it out of spite because they had tried to leave me behind. I could be a real brat. Mike always looked out for me when I was with them, but sometimes he just didn't want me around because I slowed them down.

I couldn't move as fast as the boys because I was younger. I didn't think of myself as slow and thought I could keep up with them, even though I went barefoot for most of the summer. I would wear shoes only if I had to walk a long distance, if we were in the bush, or if we went to town. Often my "home" shoes were too small for me when the nuns pulled them down from the attic. That was too bad for us, and we had to wear them home anyway; we could not take the Mission shoes. One summer, my home shoes were way too small for me, and the only pair that fit me when I got home were old tan workboots that had belonged to Mike and then Bobby. Gram dug them out of the cellar and had to soak them for a couple of days in water to soften them up. I chose not to wear them. It was not that Gram and Xp'e7e couldn't afford to buy me shoes. It was just that a trip into Williams Lake was always a big venture. I was comfortable and preferred to go without shoes. That summer we eventually did go into Williams Lake and Gram bought me a pair of canvas sneakers.

The summer that I was twelve years old, I got my menstrual period. I was so scared to tell Gram because I thought she would get mad at me. Even though that was not her nature, the time at the Mission dictated to me that even if I was innocent of something, I still felt guilty. I was scared to say anything in case I was blamed for making myself bleed. I also felt ashamed to talk about my body. I didn't know what was happening to me because the nuns at the Mission had never talked about stuff like that. The other girls did not talk to me about it either, so my first period was a traumatic time for me. I thought I might die, and yet I still couldn't make myself tell anyone. Finally, Gram found a stained pair of panties under my mattress and had a talk with me about what was happening to my body. I was so relieved to find out it was normal and that it wasn't my fault that my body was bleeding.

While we were home during the summer and Christmas holidays, Gram always tried to fatten us up. She would say, "You kids eat every-thing. You have to put on some fat before you go back to the Mission." As did all the people in my community, Gram and Xp'e7e always had lots of food to share. Every year they put in a huge vegetable garden with lots of potatoes. They dried, canned, and salted fish, moose, and deer. They had crabapple trees and cranberry bushes, just like everyone else at Soda Creek, and harvested the fruit for canning and making jelly. Gram and Xp'e7e also raised chickens, pigs, cattle, and even a few sheep. There were lots of wild rabbits and grouse and plenty of fish in the creek for a variety of meals. Along with the rest of the community, people made their yearly pilgrimage to the many lakes in the territory to harvest lake fish. All of the preserved food went into our cellar for winter use. The cellar was close to our house with two doors for winter protection. Inside the vegetables lay on the cool ground in their bins. The canned food was on shelves in the cellar. The dried food hung inside gunnysacks from the ceiling. That cellar was our grocery store. My grandparents received old-age pension cheques, but

I'm sure it was not much. Gram and Xp'e7e went into town once a month to cash their cheques and to pick up supplies from the grocery store. They bought things such as salt, coffee, sugar, macaroni, and yeast, but the majority of the good, healthy food we ate was from the bush or produced on our small farm.

Every summer, picking berries was a passion for Gram. In the spring, she would make her first round looking at the blossoms on the bushes. This told her where all the berries would be. She knew almost the exact day the berries would ripen, and off we would go to pick them. We were forever racing to get to the berry patches before the bears or before a big rain knocked the ripe berries off the bush. Sometimes we picked berries while a bear ate on the other side of the same patch. Gram gave the bear its space and, if it got too close, we left. Gram picked wild strawberries, raspberries, huckleberries, blueberries, blackberries, and soapberries. She filled the shelves of an underground cellar with all kinds of wild berry jams and she canned many bottles of the wild fruit. She also dried a lot by laying them on paper or on a blanket in the sun.

I hated picking berries. I wanted to stay and play with the other kids, but Gram wanted company in the bush. I didn't have to pick berries, I just had to go with her and keep her company, she said. Right after breakfast, we would gather up our buckets, pack a lunch, and stay out all day. We would walk or ride the horse depending on how far we were going.

One day, we were about to leave to go picking berries when Gram stepped on a nail while she was getting something inside a closet. The nail punctured her skin about an inch. I was glad, not because she hurt herself, but because I thought we wouldn't go picking berries that day. She pulled the nail out and got some soft pitch from a spruce tree, the medicine we used for burns, cuts, skin infections, and boils. Gram put some pitch on her puncture wound, bandaged her foot, and away we went.

I hated picking berries so much that while I was at the Mission I tried to make a deal with God. The priests and nuns taught us that if we wanted something, we had to pray to God for it. Some kids prayed to God to look after their families; others prayed to God to look after the less fortunate because we were told over and over again how fortunate we were that the priests and nuns were taking care of us. I must have said my prayer a million times hoping that God would one day hear me. It went like this: "Please, God, let me go to school from home. If you let me go to school from home I will willingly go picking berries with Granny."

That was the ultimate sacrifice in my little world. I was willing to pay big time so I could go to school from home. Faithfully every night I said that prayer.

Every year before we went back to the Mission, Xp'e7e would make us take buckets and go up the highway about a mile from our house to the small sawmill that operated. We would make three or four trips each with our buckets, fill them up with sawdust, bring them back to the house, and dump them into a huge container. Xp'e7e would make a paste out of the sawdust, and then we would put the paste between the logs on the house to insulate it for the winter. We did this every year. I loved the feeling of working together.

But by that time it was late summer, and those first wisps of cool autumn air meant we soon had to leave our communities again. I hated them. My mom remembers hating the smell of sweet williams blossoming in Gram's flower garden because they reminded her it was time to go back to residential school. There were other things that reminded me as an adult of my time there; for example, the sound of a distant train blowing its horn. It triggered a memory of the nights I would lie awake at the Mission and the train would roll by blowing its horn. Even though I did not know which direction it was going, I always imagined it was headed north towards Soda Creek, and I wished I were on it.

When I grew up, if anyone asked me about my childhood I would always say, "I had a great childhood." This probably surprised some people who knew of my history at residential school but, when I thought of my childhood, I only included my life at Deep Creek and Soda Creek. I did not want others to know about my years at the Mission. Those lazy, carefree days of summer were my childhood until I was reminded of the other childhood I didn't want to tell anyone about.

June 1967 was the last month I spent at the Mission. The usual excitement of going home was in the air. We had finished the school year and were waiting for Father O'Connor to come around to all the classes and read the report cards. The way they graded us was not by As, Bs, Cs, or Ds, but from best to worst student. If there were thirty-one kids in the class, we were numbered one to thirty-one. Doreen always came first and Rose Sellars usually came second, but a couple of years I managed to beat Rose and come in second ahead of Rose. Once I came eighth and felt so ashamed. I can only imagine what coming last did for other students' self-esteem. It didn't matter to me that I was at least two years younger than all the students in my class. All I knew was that I never came first, and I accepted the fact that I could never be the best. Each June, we then had the awards ceremony, where some got little statues of the Virgin Mary or other religious trinkets for good grades or behaviour. We also got a speech from Father O'Connor about going home and avoiding evils while we were away from the Mission. I couldn't imagine what evils existed in my community. Later, when Father O'Connor became bishop and was charged with numerous sexual assaults, I remembered the speeches he gave before we went home. For many of us, the evils were at the Mission.

Government policy changed in the summer of 1967, and we were finally able to go to school from home. Until that time, the schools received a per-capita grant from the government for every kid they had at the school. No kids, no money. That's what motivated the nuns and priests; they were not there to make sure everyone's rights were honoured. They were not there to respect the kids or teach positive social skills. They were simply there to herd the kids around. The only emotion that seemed to be acceptable for them to express was anger but, if we kids got caught angry and fighting, then we were punished with the strap. Violence for violence. It really was a breeding ground for dysfunction. Maybe my young age allowed me to be too impressionable, but the end result was that I believed in every way that White people were superior to "Indians." If I was walking down a sidewalk and White people came from the opposite direction I would automatically step aside to allow them to pass. I rarely looked them in the eye. I withdrew from any kind of White authority, even if I knew what they were doing was wrong. I did not know how to deal with situations I was not comfortable with, so I just withdrew. I couldn't speak up for myself. I also suffered from many phobias during my younger years. I had panic attacks if I thought I might be late for anything and I had panic attacks in new social situations. I couldn't handle even the slightest compliment or criticism with any grace. Nightmares were a regular part of my existence, and I couldn't sleep with the light out until my early thirties. Until my brother Ray died he too slept with the light on. I was scared of closed areas, and elevators especially freaked me out. I was scared of heights and of being alone. Migraine headaches were a constant companion. I enjoyed the feeling of being hungry and at one point was very skinny, even borderline anorexic. In a nutshell, I was emotionally and socially crippled in my ability to deal with the world.

Me at thirteen years old, 1968

CHAPTER 9

Summer
of '67

The summer of 1967, when I was twelve years old, was the summer many things changed in my life. It was a happy summer because Gram and Xp'e7e let me stay in town for the Williams Lake Stampede, I went to Vancouver for the first time, and the law changed, which allowed us to go to school from home. But it was also a sad summer because Xp'e7e died.

Xp'e7e still seemed healthy enough at the beginning of the summer, when he and Gram and I took the Greyhound bus into town for the Williams Lake Stampede. People came from all over for our famous stampede. In 1967, it was still a fairly small rodeo where everyone could visit and enjoy the bronco-riding and calf-tying competitions. The stampede takes place on the Canada Day weekend in early July, so each year, as soon as we got back from the Mission, our grandparents took us to the stampede. Native people from all over the Cariboo-Chilcotin and from the coast at Bella Coola, as well as tribes to the north and south, would make the trip either by horse and wagon or by car. First Nations would camp on the hills surrounding the rodeo grounds; White people would camp on the other side of the rodeo grounds. We camped with Gram and Xp'e7e at the stampede a few times. We would go by horse and wagon and pitch our tent with the rest of the Native people and take in the last two days. In what was to be Xp'e7e's last summer, we took the Greyhound bus into town because Gram and Xp'e7e had decided not to camp. They went back home on the bus after the first day, and I was allowed to stay with my friends for the full three-day event, hanging around with a group of girls but mostly with my friend Nancy Archie, from Canim Lake. We had a great time on the amusement rides and visited the different Native camps in addition to watching the rodeo and everything else there was to see. When it started to get dark on my first day at the stampede, everyone headed for "Squaw" Hall, an open-air dance hall on the outskirts of town that originally had been built for Native people, who were not welcome at the White dance hall in town. Squaw Hall had walls, a stage for the band, and some bleachers to sit on. Hilary Place and his band, the Saddle-ites, played at Squaw Hall, and some Whites came to Squaw Hall because it was so much fun. Squaw Hall was *the* place to be during the stampede. Older Native people remember the good times they had when it was just the Native people attending the dances there. By 1967, it was a drunken free-for-all and not a good place to be. A few years later, it was shut down because of all the injuries, fights, and other destructive behaviour that comes with excess alcohol. On that first night, Nancy and I waited up on the hillside by one of the campfires looking down at Squaw Hall. When we heard the music start, we headed down. The hall was packed with people bumping into each other trying to get in and people inside bumping into each other trying to dance. The majority were either drunk or well on their way to being drunk. I got scared because, up until then, alcohol had played a very small part in my life. Gram did not like it around the house, so most of the drinking done by my uncles and brothers took place in town or at other houses on the reserve. Because of all the drinking that was going on at Squaw Hall, Nancy and I decided to stand outside by the entrance to wait for her brother so she could get some money from him before he went in. While we waited, we witnessed Margaret, a Native girl in her late teens, almost forced into a car by two non-Native men. Lots of people saw it happen, but no one did anything when Margaret started screaming. She was kicking and screaming to get away from these men, and eventually managed to get away just as the two other men got out of the car to help their friends push her in. The men laughed as Margaret ran off into the hall. After seeing that, Nancy and I ran inside and stayed there until dawn when the dance ended.

I had never seen so many people, White and Indian, so drunk. I saw many kids from the Mission, and they were drunk too. The floor of the dance hall was covered with broken glass because, whenever someone finished a beer or a bottle of liquor, they would just throw it on the floor and someone would stomp on it and break it. Nancy and I sat way up in the bleachers and tried to stay out of everyone's way. One White guy who had gotten into a fight was so bloody it was scary. He had lost the fight and fallen among the broken glass on the floor. He staggered up the bleachers and sat in front of us, and I was sure he would die right there, he was so cut up. He passed out on the bleachers and was still there the next morning when we left. I saw lots of sights those two nights. During the day, Nancy and I took turns sleeping on the bleachers. One of us would take a short nap while the other would stand watch, and then we'd switch roles. We didn't get very much rest.

I was never so glad to see anyone as I was to see Gram and Xp'e7e on the third day when they came walking into the stampede grounds. They had come back to get me because, when Gram and Xp'e7e arrived home the first day of the stampede, Gram got supreme heck from my uncle Leonard. He was very upset with his parents for allowing me to stay there by myself. There were other people from Soda Creek at the stampede that I went and hung around with for a while. They fed me and watched out for me, but Leonard was right, I needed my grandparents by me to feel safe. I survived the three-day ordeal without any unpleasant consequences, but it was a real eye-opener, to say the least.

Not long after the stampede, a letter arrived from my older sister Dolly, who by this time was living in Vancouver. She had invited Mike, Bobby, and me down to stay with her for a short while. She wanted to buy us some clothes. Mike was away in Alberta with other air cadets from the Mission, and Bobby didn't want to go to Vancouver. But I decided I wanted to go to Vancouver and told Gram and Xp'e7e. They said okay and put me on the bus for Vancouver. I am sure they didn't know how big Vancouver actually was. They probably thought Vancouver was the same size as Williams Lake and that I wouldn't have any problem finding Dolly. The problem was, I went to Vancouver unannounced to my sister. All I had was a phone number. An elderly man on the bus was extremely concerned that I was going to Vancouver alone and wanted to accompany me to make sure I was okay. I did not want this White man tagging along with me, so I told him my sister would be waiting at the bus depot for me. He reluctantly got off at his stop in New Westminster, outside the city, but I'm sure he worried about me for a while after.

The Greyhound bus rolled through the outlying communities and by the time it pulled into the city bus depot, I realized Vancouver was a huge place. There were people everywhere. I phoned Dolly and luckily she was home. I don't know what I would have done if she hadn't been. If something had happened to me or if I had lost that piece of paper with her phone number on it, there would have been no way of anyone knowing for months. No one in our community had phones, so she couldn't phone anyone to see if I was coming down. Gram would never have known something had happened to me until I didn't show up in the fall for school. It's scary to think about it now, but everything turned out fine at the time, and Dolly was quite surprised to hear on the phone that I was at the bus depot in Vancouver. Her roommate's boyfriend had a car, and they came down to pick me up.

Vancouver, in the two weeks I was there, was quite an experience for me. Dolly shared an apartment with two other girls near English Bay, a beautiful part of the city. Dolly worked days in the office at Indian Medical Services, so I was left on my own to explore. The first morning, I found two dollars on the table with a note that Dolly had left for me. That was a lot of money to me, and I bought oranges, grapes, and bananas. Fruit was something I didn't get much of, and I had not developed a taste for candy. My system was not used to sweets.

I explored Vancouver on my own and had a great time doing it. Every day, I would take a sheet of paper with me when I went out and make my own map wherever I went. I knew nothing of city maps, streets, or numbers, so I worked out a simple system of my own. If I went two blocks east, I would mark the two blocks on my sheet of paper; if I turned north and walked another three blocks, I marked it on my map and so on. I spent my days exploring and went what I thought to be long distances. When I wanted to go back, I simply retraced my steps from the map and I would end up back at Dolly's place.

The neatest thing I remember about Vancouver was buying popcorn from a vendor down by the beach at English Bay. I went home and told my brothers about how I could buy popcorn from this man with a huge popcorn machine that he rolled on wheels on the sidewalk by the beach. They didn't believe me, and I couldn't convince them I was telling the truth. At home, the only way we had ever made popcorn was in a small pot on our wood stove.

Dolly topped the trip off for me by taking me to a western clothing store and buying me some new clothes. My uncles always bought the magazine *Western Horseman*, and in the magazine beautiful girls modelled western outfits. I would go through the magazines page by page looking at the clothes and imagining myself dressed in the fringed shirts and jeans the girls wore. Although my clothes weren't exactly like the ones in the magazine, it felt pretty good walking around wearing brand-new western clothes. Except for the outfit the nurses bought me when I left Sardis, these were probably the only store-bought clothes I ever had. Soon after that, Dolly and I caught a ride home to Deep Creek with her friend from a neighbouring community.

My mother came to visit not long after my return from Vancouver, and I was invited to go with her and Lawrence and their four children down to Summerland. I did, and while I was down there, Xp'e7e died. It happened when Xp'e7e and Gram were riding home from picking berries. They were on our horse, Loco, with Gram in front. When they were just across the creek from the house, Gram felt Xp'e7e slump against her but didn't think anything of it because, after a long day, she thought he must be tired. She knew something was wrong, however, when the bucket of berries he was holding dumped. She stopped the horse, dismounted, managed to get Xp'e7e onto the ground, and went running home to get help. My uncles, Johnny and Leonard, and my brother Ray ran to bring Xp'e7e across the creek and back to the house. Uncle Johnny then got on the horse and went galloping down to the store, about a mile away, to use the phone to call an ambulance. He then rode back to the house, and they waited for the ambulance. It was taking too long, so my brother Ray got on the horse and, again, went to call the ambulance. He returned, and they waited some more. My grandmother was heading down to the store to call the ambulance for the third time when my uncle Johnny caught up to her at the end of our driveway. He told Gram that Xp'e7e was really bad and that she had better go back to the house. By the time she got to Xp'e7e's bedside, he was dead. When my brother Ray and my uncle Leonard gave Gram the bad news, she cried, "No!" and ran to get some holy water she had gotten from the priest. She splashed it on Xp'e7e, hoping that it would somehow bring him back to life.

Gram said that the ambulance, which should have taken no more than twenty minutes to travel from Williams Lake, finally came at eight in the evening, five hours after the original call. They took Xp'e7e to the hospital in the ambulance, and the doctor later told Gram that Xp'e7e had died from a massive heart attack. I've often wondered whether they could have saved him or, at least, made his last few hours a little less painful. They could also have saved Gram, my uncles, and my brother the unnecessary stress of waiting for the ambulance to come.

My family made no complaint about the unacceptable time it took for the ambulance to get to Deep Creek. There was no explanation from the ambulance driver about why it took so long. That's just the way things were in White-Native relationships at the time. As Natives, we were all well programmed not to complain. We knew any complaints would have fallen on deaf ears. We were powerless.

In a similar incident at Soda Creek a few years later, Clarney Michel fell asleep in bed with his cigarette and nearly burned to death. My mom used to always visit down at the Michels and found Clarney in bed in tremendous pain. The only person on the rez who had a phone was Laura Phillips. We called the ambulance in the early evening. We waited. We called again and were rudely told it would be out there. We waited. There were no cars in our community to bring Clarney to the hospital. One of the women from our community, Addie Sellars, stayed with Clarney and tried to make him as comfortable as possible throughout the night. The next afternoon, a Sunday, the ambulance came driving in as if they were on a leisurely drive. A few of us were on the road headed out of the reserve. The guy on the passenger side said sarcastically, "We heard somebody got burnt around here. You know anything about it?" We were upset that Clarney spent the night suffering but, of course, we didn't say anything to the ambulance crew. We pointed them to the house and, again, we made no complaint to anyone. They took Clarney to the hospital, where he stayed for months getting treatment for his burns. He recovered but, years later, ended up freezing to death during the winter.

When my mom and I got the news that Xp'e7e had died, we caught the bus to Soda Creek. Along the way, we had to stop in the community of Salmon Arm and, while we were there, she bought me a triangle pendant with the town's name on it. Handing it to me, she said, "Here, you always keep this." I thought that was a strange thing for her to do, but I didn't ask any questions. I took it home with me. Years later, when I was in my thirties, Mom finally told me about my biological father and how she had met him. My mom had been walking out of Soda Creek, trying to get away from her first husband, Michel, who had beaten her up. A White guy stopped and offered her a ride. He had a friendly face, something she probably appreciated after the beating, and she ended up going to Kamloops with him. They stayed overnight, and then he had to go to Salmon Arm. He paid for another night, gave Mom five dollars, and told her to wait for him. She didn't wait. She took the five dollars and caught the bus back to Williams Lake. Little did she know she was carrying me. When I was born, Angelique Sellars came to see Mom in the hospital in Williams Lake. She took one look at my fair skin and said, "Oh, oh … *somebody's* been messin' around." Angelique was a good friend to Mom and she was my godmother. My cousin June once remarked when I told her that her mom was my godmother, "No wonder she had such a soft spot for you!"

It used to bother me that I did not know who my biological father was, until I realized that it isn't so much where you came from but what you do when you get here. Even though I don't know the identity of my biological father, I bear my mom no animosity. Once I got into an abusive relationship of my own, I fully understood her flight from abuse. I am just so grateful for being born, and I'm glad Mom was able to find a friend when she needed one.

The Greyhound bus that took Mom and me to Xp'e7e's funeral arrived at Soda Creek about five in the morning, and we walked down the hill towards the village. The sun was up and burning off the morning mist that covered the valley. It was a beautiful day, but I could feel a sense of dread the closer we got to the village. The thought of Xp'e7e being dead scared me. We went to one of the houses in the village and asked after Xp'e7e. Mom thought they would have him at Soda Creek, but we found out he was at Deep Creek, so we caught a ride back to Deep Creek. Gram saw Mom first and, after speaking to her, asked where I was. I was hiding behind some other people, not wanting to play any part in this. They put me in front of them so Gram could see me. She called me over and held me. That was one of only two times she ever held me when I was older. The other time was when my uncle Johnny died.

Preparations for my grandfather's funeral were frightening for me. Our traditional custom dictated that children were not allowed near dead bodies. I had never seen a dead body before, so when Gram brought me to Xp'e7e's body to say goodbye to him it was very traumatic for me. I kept thinking about the commercials I saw on TV about mouth-to-mouth resuscitation, and I wanted someone to try it on Xp'e7e and maybe he would come back to life. I wished I could ask someone to try it but, because of my insecurities, I was scared even at that crucial time that someone would laugh at me. So instead I cried and cried. Later, I asked Gram if I could go and stay with my cousin Phyllis. For the first time in my life, I didn't want to be around Xp'e7e. Gram said I could spend the night with Phyllis up at Percy and Angelique's place. Phyllis and I were both very young, but she seemed to know more about death than I did and she knew what to say to comfort me. I stayed away from Gram's house when Xp'e7e's body was there before the funeral, and even though I must have attended, I don't remember the funeral itself. After that, a deep sadness set on our family. We all sat around lost in our own space. After the daily chores were done, a silence settled over the house only to be broken by someone clearing their throat or shifting their position in a chair. Every morning for months, I woke to hear Gram quietly crying but, as soon as she heard a movement in the house, the crying stopped. For a year, Gram wore depressing, black clothing. Then one day she came out with a bright dress and announced, "It is time for the mourning to be over." I felt kind of sad, because acknowledging that the mourning was over was like finally acknowledging that Xp'e7e really wasn't coming back.

The other significant thing that happened in the summer of 1967 was that I found out I would be able to go to school from home. Early that summer, before Xp'e7e died, Father O'Connor had come to see

Gram. It was unusual, because even though other priests came on a regular basis, Father O'Connor had never been to our house before. He told us not to get our hopes up, but we might be able to go to school from home. I can still feel that surge of excitement thinking of the possibility of living at home while going to school. By the end of the summer, we found out a final decision had been made and we were allowed to go to school from home. That year, 1967, was the last year the Mission was funded per student; instead, it started to receive grants from the government to cover expenses no matter how many kids were enrolled. All of a sudden, the nuns and priests didn't feel the need to round up as many kids as possible, and the number of kids enrolled at the Mission dropped dramatically. Even though it was a very sad time in our house, I was ecstatic we would finally be allowed to stay with our families. From the time I was five years old until I was twelve, I had only been in my community for a total of eleven months: two weeks at Christmas break and two months during the summer.

In the fall of 1967, I entered grade eight at Williams Lake Junior Secondary. I didn't think much about it during the summer but, about a week before school started, Gram said we had to go get school supplies. I thought she knew what we would need, so we went to town. It wasn't long before we both realized that Gram didn't know what I needed and neither did I. It was only then that it struck me that I would be going to school with Whites, and I felt a panic rising because I didn't know how I was ever going to measure up. They were perfect in every way, and here I was, an Indian, a big mark against me already, and now I didn't even know what supplies I would need to go to school. By this time in my young life, little things that others would not bat an eye at gave me panic attacks. I was so scared of doing anything wrong and, without proper supplies, it seemed to me that I would surely be in trouble or, worse, ridiculed. That may sound silly but, when you have been told what to do, when to do it, and how to do it in an institution for so many years, you lack the capability to make even the smallest decision.

Stories told by the older girls from the Mission who had gone on to the high school in town only made my fears grow. It was obvious from the stories that White kids didn't think much of Indians. The only time I had ever seen so many White kids together in one place was in the spring of 1967 when a group of them came to visit the Mission. The nun told us that we would be getting some company, but we had to stay away from them. A while later, a busload of White girls came to the school. It was centennial year for them, and they were dressed in the old-time garb, long dresses, and bonnets that they wore often during their celebration year. The girls got off the bus and went into the main building. I don't know what they were doing there. We were kept outside and watched from a distance. The thing I remember most is how noisy they were. They laughed, some squealed, and they talked and skipped down the sidewalk. I watched with curiosity and thought how odd they were.

Even though some of us could finally go to school from home, we were not allowed to ride on the same buses as the White kids. The Department of Indian Affairs hired Mr. and Mrs. Wilson to bus the Aboriginal kids from Soda Creek and Deep Creek to and from school. They were okay people. Mrs. Wilson drove the bus to begin with. She didn't say much. Later they hired a guy by the name of "Red" to drive the bus. They drove an old school bus that backfired on a regular basis, especially when we were going downhill just outside the Williams Lake Junior Secondary School. We also left a trail of blue smoke from the exhaust to alert others where we had been. I had heard of Indians and smoke signals, but that was ridiculous. The bus probably should have been in the junkyard, but I guess they thought it was good enough for the Indian kids. All the other buses had "School District No. 27" written on the side. Ours said in big letters, "Cache Creek Motors." The other kids called it "The Indian Bus." My cousin Edie (Sellars) Woods would lie down on the seat so no one would see her through the window and then she would try to sneak off the bus when it stopped to let us off for our day at school. Then at the end of the day, there was our battered old bus among all the other school buses. Even the kids who were still at the Mission had better buses.

During one of our bus trips to school, the back tire came off just as we were going around a corner. Luckily, we had just gotten off the highway and were not going too fast. None of us were hurt badly except for a boy in the back, Chuck (Gilbert) Sellars, who injured his arm and shoulder. He must have been in a lot of pain because he was crying, and usually Chuck did not cry. They didn't take him to the hospital. He was able to walk and, like the rest of us, completed the ten-minute walk to the school. We thought maybe we would get a new bus but, after school that afternoon, there came the Cache Creek Motors bus, backfiring and smoking into the schoolyard. The driver said they put the wheel back on and that was it. They never did change the sign on the side of the bus to read "School District No. 27." The sign just always stayed "Cache Creek Motors." We eventually did get a newer, but not brand-new, bus, but they squeezed every ounce of mileage out of that old bus for a couple more years. The newer bus did not have anything written on the side.

I know Mr. and Mrs. Wilson didn't have to follow the regulations of other school buses because they also used the school bus as a taxi for the older people on the reserve. They charged each adult two dollars for a ride into town and two dollars for a ride back. Sometimes in the afternoon, we would get on the bus and our relatives would be on the same bus drunk, or fighting, or both. All we could do was try to hide our intense embarrassment and hope that all the kids came out of school right away so we could get the hell out of the schoolyard. I was always so conscious of the other kids looking at our bus and laughing. As much as we loved our relatives, it was quite embarrassing. No one else had older people on their buses, and no one else had people drinking on their buses. But, as embarrassing as it was, I still preferred to ride that old bus from home with all the shame that came with it than ride a newer bus from the Mission.

Kids did things at the public school that we would have gotten a good strapping for at the Mission. They would mouth off to the teachers or walk away from them while the teacher was still talking. At first I was scared for the White kids because I thought they were going to get a good beating. I soon saw that they could get away with a lot before they even got in trouble. Some were sent down to the principal's office, but they didn't seem too upset when they came back. It amazed me.

I didn't have or want any White friends. I just wanted to be left alone with my Indian friends. There were White kids who did try to be friendly, but many made it clear they wanted nothing to do with the Indian kids. We tried to stay out of their way. We had our own little circles, and there were no White kids in our group and no Indian kids in the White groups. I hung around with the kids who came into public school but lived at the Mission. We would bring deer-meat and moose-meat sandwiches on homemade bread for the Mission students to exchange for small amounts of money or something else they might have. That created a problem with some kids who had nothing to trade for our sandwiches. They became jealous because we no longer had to go to the Mission, and we had something they didn't have. The Mission dysfunction carried on to high school. A girl who was a rival of mine at the Mission succeeded in turning many of the junior high-school girls away from me now that I was considered an outsider. Those same girls would have sided with me over her, as they had many times before, but now I was able to go to school from home and somehow that made me different. It was like the shoes thing. I started hanging around with Native kids from other communities who were going to school from home.

It was during my first year at public school that I discovered that White people could be stupid. It shocked me because the idea of a White person being stupid was something that totally went against everything I had been taught. I was shocked when a White person would come to school with torn or dirty clothes. In every way, before I started to see through the myths, I thought they were perfect.

I was in a cooking class. We were in groups of two and my partner was a White girl. We had been partners since the class started, but we didn't talk much, mostly because I sent off strong vibes of not wanting to engage with her. If she tried to talk to me, I would answer her with as short a reply as possible; usually, I just said yes or no. She talked to the other girls, but I tried not to pay any attention to them. I did notice they kind of shunned her though. One day, she started yakking away to me. I can't remember what it was she was saying, but I do remember we were making apple crisp. At the end of the class, when we sat down to eat our baked dessert, it occurred to me that maybe I was smarter than this girl. That was a totally new concept for me. It just didn't seem possible that she could be White and so dumb, and that she could say such stupid things. After that realization, I began to listen to her and even ask a few questions. As the year progressed, I lost any feelings of intimidation being around her. I even felt a slight superiority over her. I knew I was smarter than she was, but that feeling only extended to her, and I thought she must be the exception to the rule about Whites being smarter. I still thought, because I was Indian, I was not as smart as White people.

Something else that shocked me was the way the White girls were so open with their bodies. After our gym class, the White girls would have showers and not bother to cover up with a towel or hide behind curtains while they dressed. They sometimes even compared breasts, stomachs, and legs. I was quite amazed at that. I would go behind the curtain and make sure it was completely closed with no peek holes where someone could walk by and catch a glimpse of me. I was always so conscious of what I saw as my imperfect body. When I showered, it was only when no one else was around, and it was a very quick dip in and out so no one would catch me without any clothes on.

Sometimes on my lunch hours in that grade-eight year, I went to the gym to watch the White kids practise their school sports. I always wanted to play on the basketball, volleyball, or some other school sports teams, but there were no Indian kids on the school teams, and

I didn't have the courage to try to be the first one. Instead, I would just go and watch and be as close to the sports events as I dared to be.

A White girl who played on one of the teams saw me watching them and told me I should try out for the team. I told her I took the bus after school, and since it was a requirement to stay after for practice, I wouldn't have a ride home. She told me to go talk to the school counsellor and maybe she would be able to help me find a ride home after practice. I had passed the counsellor's office about ten times a day, but I never knew what she did. I saw White kids sitting in her office, so I assumed she was a teacher of sorts, but I didn't really think about her actual role in the school. It surprised me that she could possibly help me if I wanted to play on one of the teams. There were a few reasons I didn't go see her. First, she was a White authority figure, and my training from the Mission told me not to ask for anything. Second, because I was Native, I didn't think she'd want to help me anyway. Third, I didn't know whether I could handle being around all White kids. I did try to join a noon-hour badminton game. I went once but felt too uncomfortable around all those White kids.

When we went to grade eight from the Mission, the priests, the school district, or maybe a combination of both thought we weren't smart enough to handle the academic program, so they enrolled us in the pre-vocational program. There were no Aboriginal kids in the pre-academic program and, of course, I just did as I was told, did not question anything, and went along with what others had decided for me.

When I was in grade nine, my homeroom teacher stopped me in the hallway to tell me how excited he was because I had one of the top scores on an IQ test. I knew I had done something good, but I wasn't sure what such a test was and I didn't want to ask him because I didn't want him to think I was stupid. A few years later, when I finally found out about IQ tests, I understood my teacher's excitement and it made me feel pretty darn good. I took another test in college and scored 133, and I am told only 2 percent of the population score that high. IQ tests are controversial, and today I don't put much faith in them, but just scoring that high gave me such a sense of self-worth. I wish I had summoned the courage to ask about the IQ test in high school. It would have had a very positive effect on my life. Smarter than most kids in that school! Smarter than most of the White kids in that school! Whoa! That would have blown me away.

Grade nine was the year I got straight As in math. I had a crush on the teacher, Mr. Scheck. I was very shy, but I managed to raise my hand when I knew the answer and would try to forget that there were thirty other kids in the class. Our paths crossed years later on the Williams Lake golf course. He was playing a round of golf with my husband, Bill, and he asked, "You remember who I am, don't you?" I just smiled as I said, "Yes, I do." I think those were the only As I got, except for courses you really had to work at to fail, like typing or shorthand.

Grade nine was the year we had to decide whether we were going on the academic or vocational program. We each had an individual session with the school counsellor. When it was my turn to see her, she asked which program I wished to go in. I asked her, "What's the difference between the academic and vocational programs?" Her answer to me was, "In the vocational program you don't have to take French." That's the only explanation she gave me. She sat looking at me after that explanation waiting for an answer. I had taken French in grade eight and didn't really care to take it again, even though Mr. Poulton made the course enjoyable. He helped us remember French words using humour. "Derrière" means "behind" in English. He said, "Mrs. Poulton has a big derrière." Even though I liked Mr. Poulton, I chose the vocational program because I was not keen on taking French.

When I reached grade ten, I went to Columneetza Senior Secondary in Williams Lake. Leona Meldrum and I were paired up to be partners in our science class. We immediately became friends but got frustrated at a project and didn't get the help we needed, so we just quit working. We went to class but sat and talked. If we were making too much noise, our science teacher, Mr. Stewart, would come over and tell us to quiet down. Other than that, he didn't bother about trying to make us do any work. Leona and I failed the class, but we became best friends.

It was through Leona that I got to know a few White girls from the Riske Creek area. Leona lived with her aunt and uncle at Meldrum Creek, which is close to Riske Creek. A group of White girls from the surrounding area hung around together. Noreen, Sharon, and Iris are the ones I remember. They were the first White people I had encountered who I felt comfortable with. They were the first White kids in the public school who were my friends. We weren't close, and I wasn't part of their group, but I felt all right going over and sitting with them if they were in the cafeteria or on the lawn outside. I enjoyed being around them, and I was learning that I shouldn't expect to be treated as an inferior by all White people.

Grade ten was the year I had Mr. Wiebe as a social studies teacher. He surprised me in one class by raising the subject of residential schools. I didn't realize the destruction that the schools inflicted at the time. Mr. Wiebe started talking about residential schools, and he got really angry. He asked the non-Native kids, "How would you like to be taken away from your parents and sent to a school for years at a time?" Then he asked each Native kid in the class how many years we went there. I was embarrassed. I can now appreciate the anger Mr. Wiebe was feeling after I realized the damage the schools have done, but I honestly couldn't understand at the time why he, a White person, was getting so upset about the residential schools.

My cousin Lenny said Mr. Wiebe helped him take a different look at the way Native people are portrayed. Mr. Wiebe pointed out in his social studies class that when there were wars between the Whites and Natives, it was always a victory when the White people won and a massacre when the Indians won. That helped Lenny look at what White people were saying about Indians in a different way, and he realized that it was unfair the way Native people are portrayed.

CHAPTER 10

Life
on the
Reserve

Grade nine was the year I noticed Mike and Bobby staying out all weekend and drinking. I was surprised Gram didn't say anything to them because she was so strict with me. I was thirteen, and the only place I was allowed to go, except for school, was to check for mail down at the store. Gram didn't want me around with my friends and cousins on the reserve, who were into drinking by this time. I obeyed Gram for a while, but I hated spending weekends and evenings by myself. The problem was that "kids my age" who had been in the same classroom with me for years were actually two to four years older than me. I was hanging around with kids who were sixteen to eighteen years old. When they taunted me to stay in town with them on Fridays, I soon succumbed to peer pressure. It did not help that I had physically developed early and looked older than I was.

By the time I was fourteen, I was not listening to Gram, and it eventually resulted in me getting a beating from my uncle Leonard. I had stayed with my cousin Rose Sellars for a dance at our community hall, and the Deep Creek dances had a reputation for being wild. It shocked me to see a few of our teachers from Columneetza there but, again, that was when I still saw the world through the tunnel vision of the Mission. The dances eventually got so out of hand that the RCMP shut them down for good. There were stabbings, car crashes, assaults, and everything else that comes with excessive drinking.

I was at one of these dances, it was late, and Percy Sellars Sr. who had been at the dance stopped by Gram's house on the way home and told her I was there and that I was drinking. Uncle Ernie and Gram came down to the hall and yarded me out of there. The next day, she and Leonard tried to make me promise I would stay home. I wouldn't and Leonard tried to beat me into submission. He kept shaking and slapping me and tried to make me say that I would listen. I kept saying no. After what seemed like hours, but was probably only ten to fifteen minutes, he gave up. It was then that Gram told me I would have to go and live with my mother. I started packing. She asked me what I was doing and I told her I was moving out. She says, "You'll stay here until your mother gets here!"

After I left Gram's house and moved to Soda Creek with Mom and Lawrence, I started to drink with family members and other people on the reserve. I was shocked when we went to the liquor store and Lawrence asked me, "What kind of beer do you want, Bev?" I was only fourteen years old. Gram would have had a fit if she heard that. I knew it was wrong, but having Lawrence's approval made it okay. I didn't drink all the time but on a fairly regular basis.

I was in grade ten and making an effort to go to school. I had no desire to drop out, although I wasn't doing as well as I could have. One Friday afternoon, my cousin Rose wanted to go downtown and she asked me to go with her. I told her, "No, I've just about made it a whole week without missing any days." Rose laughed at me and went downtown on her own, but I stayed and, for at least that one week during high school, I attended a whole week of classes.

There were other reasons I missed school. Sometimes I would be up half the night driving Lawrence and his friends to a bootlegger in Williams Lake. When they were drinking and ran out of booze, I was their designated driver. Lawrence didn't like to drive when he drank, so he would wake me up. It didn't matter what time of the night it was, Lawrence would wake me up saying, "Come on, Bev, get up. We have to go to a bootlegger." I tried to get out of it by using an excuse like I had to go to school the next morning but it didn't matter. He wouldn't leave me alone until I got up and drove them to the bootlegger. I never worried about not having a driver's licence because I was stopped a few times by the RCMP but always got away with just a warning. Once at about midnight, I was stopped on our way home after everyone came out of the beer parlour. There were probably six or seven people in the car, all of them pretty intoxicated. Lawrence told the RCMP officer that he was teaching me how to drive. At that hour, I was shocked when the officer let us go. I guess he thought it was easier to let me take everyone home. Although I started to drive when I was fourteen, I didn't get a licence until I was twenty-three years old.

I learned how to drive a standard going to the bootlegger. I had been disappointed when Lawrence and Mom had gone to Vancouver to buy a car and came home with a standard rather than an automatic gearshift. At that time, I did not know how to shift gears. Oh well, I thought, the silver lining was that I would not be dragged out of bed in the middle of the night to drive to the bootlegger. Not long after getting the car, Lawrence came and woke me up. I said, "No, I don't know how to drive a standard." "Come on, Bev, get up, I'll teach you," Lawrence said. I groaned as I always did when I had to get up in the middle of the night. Lawrence sat me behind the wheel and showed me how to work the clutch and gearshift. By the time we had reached Williams Lake, some twenty-three miles away, I could drive pretty well. So that's how I learned to drive a stick shift, in the middle of the night, taking a carload of drunks to the bootlegger. On such excursions, we would sometimes go see the bootlegger and return home but, other times, Lawrence wanted to visit someone. We would wake people up in the middle of the night and they would drink together. He always knew who would need a drink in the middle of the night. Alcoholics know how other alcoholics function, and Lawrence was always welcomed. I would usually try to get some sleep in the car until we were ready to go home. I almost always made it to school the next day.

When I was sixteen, I went to Prince George to do part of grade twelve at Prince George College. I was having a tough time getting to school in Williams Lake, and I knew if I didn't get away I would not finish. Nothing was going to get in my way of becoming a nurse and I was going to finish high school. Prince George College was a Catholic school. The majority of kids were Aboriginal, but there were a number of White kids attending the school. One day I was in my shorthand class, and the teacher asked me, "What are you going to do after you graduate, Bev?" I didn't have to think about the answer. I knew from the time I met Miss Costello at Sardis that I was going to be a nurse. By the age of ten, I would study a medical book my uncle Leonard had so I could get a head start on my nurse's training. When the teacher asked me what I hoped to be, I replied, "I'm going to be a nurse." She said, "You can't be a nurse; you're not on the academic program." She then fully explained the difference between the academic and vocational programs and told me I should have been taking science courses from grade nine. I literally could feel the wind being taken out of my sail. My hopes of becoming a nurse were dashed. I lost interest in school and ended up quitting five months before I was to graduate. I had moved to Prince George so I would make sure to graduate. After that, my attitude was, "Why bother?" It didn't matter to me whether I graduated. The funny thing is that when I told my family and community members that I had quit school, it was like telling them I had a ham sandwich for lunch. There was no shock or worry. It was sort of like it was expected of me. I did hear through the grapevine, or the moccasin telegraph, as I like to call it, that Gram was pretty upset that I had quit, but she never did tell me to my face.

After quitting school at sixteen, I was pulled more and more into the party scene. When you lived on the rez, it was an accepted part of life. One evening, I had gone over to visit some community members, Mop and Freddy Sampson. Mop's real name was Margaret Pop, but everyone called her "Mop." They had just come from town, and Mop had brought some beer that was set in the middle of the living room. "Do you want a beer, Bev?" she asked. Without even thinking, I said, "Yeah," and grabbed for the beer. While I was reaching for it, somehow the thought came to me, "Geez, Bev, *how easily* you reach for that beer." It was like a slap in the face. All of a sudden, I was so conscious of my actions. Maybe it was Gram's never-ending lectures about the evils of alcohol that decided to click in right then or maybe it was something "beyond" that was trying to guide me. All I know is that while I was reaching for that beer, I experienced an epiphany that would change the way I viewed drinking.

I thought about the place I would end up if I continued to drink with everyone on the rez. No one drank socially in our community at that time. It was blackout binging or nothing. There was no happy medium, probably because people used alcohol to dull their senses. I thought about the things that happen to people when they drink. Since moving out of my grandparents' place, I had seen things that happened at parties and did not want any part of it. All these thoughts just tumbled through my mind. I told Mop, "No, I don't think I *will* have one." After that, I still drank but nowhere near as often as I did in the two years previous. I even resorted to "taking a pledge" from the Catholic church not to drink. It seemed to be the only way people would leave you alone. Otherwise, the ones trying to quit drinking would be given a rough time for not drinking with the rest of the crowd. "What? You think you're too good to drink with us?" was a common response if I turned down their offer of a drink. The fear of the church was still strong, so saying, "I have taken the pledge" ensured you were left alone and not badgered to drink.

When I was sixteen years old, I met the man who would become my husband and the father of my children. The first time I met Dayton Mack, he was out with one of my relatives at a Sugar Cane dance. He was popular among the women around Williams Lake, and we began going out once in a while before I moved to Prince George. He came up once to visit but didn't stay long. Then he came to visit again a few months later, and I decided to leave Prince George with him and go back to Soda Creek. By that time, I had learned I couldn't become a nurse.

Once I got back to Soda Creek, Dayton was a regular visitor and, just before my seventeenth birthday, he moved in with us. We stayed with Mom and Lawrence for a short while before we got a place of our own in the community. That surprised me because, when they weren't drinking, they didn't like anyone staying with us. I think Lawrence was looking to get rid of some responsibility, to be specific, me. I heard him talking to Dayton about me, trying to convince him that I was a good catch. He said, "Bev is a good worker. She's strong." I felt like a horse on the auction block and wanted to ask if they needed to see my teeth as well.

I *was* strong. I could pack fish on my back up the steep banks of the Fraser River with the best of them. But then, I did not have a choice about going fishing. Because Lawrence was White, he needed someone with an Indian status card to be with him whenever he was fishing in traditional First Nations territory. It was a tough life at times, but I had to go when told because they were supporting me. We would fish at night because the river rocks got too hot during the day and the fish would easily spoil when we set them on the rocks to fish some more. As daylight broke, we began to pack the salmon up the steep hillsides to the car. We then would sell the fish to Lawrence's fish buyers, and then go right back to the river to catch more fish. I would get pretty tired because, when the fish were running, we would be down the river every night. Gram did not like to hear that I was out there selling fish. She gave me heck for doing that on one of my visits to see her. I had been down the river lots of times with Gram and Xp'e7e, but I never had to pack salmon, and they did not sell it. Gram dried, canned, or salted the salmon they got.

Fishing season was always a time of great excitement. Throwing the first fish caught into a pot of boiling water was the highlight of fishing season. Everyone kept an ear to the ground about the first fish coming up the river. The moccasin telegraph was pretty accurate and so we knew where the fish were most times and how many days it would take to get to us. When they did arrive, not only did we get our winter's supply of fish, but it was also the summer social event and, even if you weren't fishing, the river was the place to be. People would pack their coffee, flashlight, sacks, and net, and head to the river. If the fish were not running in great numbers, people would wander around to other fishing sites to visit and share a coffee. I loved being down the river during fishing season and was pretty much a "river rat" during my teens until my mid-thirties. I spent many, many nights along the Fraser River and at Farewell Canyon at the traditional fishing places of the Secwepemc people.

In addition to helping Lawrence pack fish, I also helped him and others pull out numerous moose and deer from the bush. And I was never idle when we were out bringing in the winter's supply of wood. I did more than my share of domestic chores. Because I worked hard, I suppose I was considered a good catch.

My relationship with Dayton was full of troubles right from the beginning. I entered the relationship eagerly, but it was not long before I realized that being with him offered more pain than happiness. Fifteen years went by before I would finally break free. To be fair to Dayton, not everything about the relationship was bad. We did have some good times, although they were few and far between. The best thing about our relationship was our three children.

I had been on the receiving end of violence for most of my early life, not all the time but enough to have a negative effect on me. That finally ended when I was in my early thirties and my marriage dissolved. I finally got a restraining order against Dayton. I went to the RCMP after one of his battering incidents and filled out a form. I was then told I would have to go to court but the police didn't tell me any more than that. I went to court the day I was given only to find the place was packed and many of the people in there knew both Dayton and me. When our names were called, I was horrified that they read aloud the statement I had made to the RCMP. The judge asked Dayton whether the serious accusations I had made against him were true. Dayton admitted they were. The restraining order was granted but I left the courtroom that day with such shame. I assumed the hearing would take place in private and never meant for our dirty laundry to be aired in public. The violence began with the years I spent at the Mission. Physical abuse became an accepted way of life for me. The nuns and some of the other kids contributed to it. This prepared me to step right into an abusive relationship with my husband. The first time I was beat up, the thought of leaving him just did not occur to me. Many of the other women in the community were going through the same thing. It was normal, and one couple even called the bruises on the woman "love bruises." I didn't like being beat up, but I accepted it without complaining. It was when I left my grandmother's home that physical abuse from other family members started. When they were drinking and their frustrations came out, they vented on those close to them. Sometimes I was the closest.

I look back at all of this now and see how the destruction of our culture and utter hopelessness were expressed in the form of violence. Suicides were sometimes "the answer" when things got too tough. If I could get a list of all those I went to school with at the Mission and if I looked at the number of those who committed suicide or had violent deaths, I am sure the percentage would be high.

I did have that one suicide attempt, the incident with which I began my story, and, obviously, I was unsuccessful. And what incident triggered that attempt? I was at a house in Sugar Cane when one of the owners told me that a girl who Dayton was seeing behind my back wondered whether I knew about their affair. Of course, I knew! But that statement took me over the edge.

It turns out that before I went to lie down and die, I told the lady of the house that I had taken the pills. I have no memory of telling her, but I do remember lying on the bed thinking I would soon exit this world. Apparently, she told Lawrence that I had taken the pills. They tried to wake me up and couldn't, so Lawrence took me to the hospital where my stomach was pumped.

I was surprised to wake up in the hospital. When I woke up, the White nurse who was attending to me was mean. She made my short stay miserable. "You people!" I remember her angrily saying. Even though I was still shaky, as soon as the tubes were taken out of me, I found my clothes, but couldn't find my shoes. I left the hospital without them. Instead of having compassion, which is what I needed then, the White nurse made me feel like I was so stupid that I couldn't even kill myself properly. Maybe that is what she was pissed off about, that I had not been successful. What is that saying I have heard a number of times? "The only good Indian is a dead Indian."

I walked out of that hospital and up to the highway, and I had every intention of walking home. I wasn't out of the city limits yet when my brother Ray and Lloyd Sellars came along in Lloyd's truck. Ray had heard what I had done and, in the only way he knew that showed he cared what happened to me, he gave me supreme heck for trying to commit suicide. "God damn you, Bevie, what the hell did you do that for?" is a good approximation of what he said to me. I didn't try to offer an explanation. I didn't know why I did it. I just knew I wanted out. I sat in the truck between him and Lloyd and waited till Ray had finished giving me heck; then he said, "I'm taking you to Granny's. You damn well better stay there for a while too." I didn't argue. I needed to be around Gram right then. When Lloyd and Ray dropped me at Gram's, she didn't let on that she knew. We never hugged. She didn't ask me if anything was wrong. She just provided the comfort of having her near me when I needed it. During the years that followed, until her death in 1997, every time I needed comfort I would go and stay with Gram. She seemed to sense when I was troubled and gave me my space. She never asked questions. She would just let me be. I would stay, and just her presence always made me strong enough to go out and face the world again. Suicide seemed to be always lurking in my mind and there were a couple of other times I made half-assed attempts to end my life. Once while I was talking to Mom at our house in Soda Creek, I decided to take a whole pile of Aspirin. Neither of us was drinking. I remember not wanting to be around. It had nothing to do with Mom. It had more to do with my life in general. I remember even laughing while Mom and I were talking, and I did not let on that I had taken anything. As I went to sleep, I wondered if I would wake up, and it didn't bother me if I didn't. I didn't bother mentioning it to anyone because it just didn't seem an issue at the time.

I also have telltale scars from slicing my left arm, something I have noticed in other Aboriginal women. I was with Dayton when that happened. We were drinking with a group of people and then we gave someone a ride out to Alkali Lake. Along the way back into town, we stopped along the side of the road, and I went and sat on the bank of the road by myself. There was a piece of broken glass beside me where I sat. I picked it up and started to slash my wrists and forearms. I was not arguing with anyone and there didn't seem to be any rational reason why I would do that. I didn't know why I did it. Dayton saw me and came running over. He got a shirt, wrapped my arm, and asked me to tell him why I would do that. All I could do was cry. I had no answers. Now when I look back, I see that I felt an extreme sadness in my soul, and a simple piece of glass that happened to be where I sat offered what I saw as an out for me. I did not like the world I lived in and existed in one day at a time. I was mentally ill because my experiences to that point had been so negative. Over the years, whenever anyone, even my kids, asked me about the scars on my wrists and forearms I always said I got them while fencing our fields.

CHAPTER 11

One Day I
Realized
I Had
Survived

One day I woke up and realized I was well into my twenties. It surprised me that I had survived. In my youth, I always felt I would not live to an age beyond my teens. To us, the lives we led were normal because we had no other experiences to compare, but others saw the oppression and darkness of our lives, even if we didn't. I remember a few White people coming to our reserve with some of our members who had married non-Aboriginal men. They were looking around the reserve and studying the people who lived there. At the time, we were playing softball at Soda Creek, something we did on a regular basis. I was sitting on the bench beside a White woman when she commented, "How can they laugh? How can they have fun?" I was shocked by her question. It was only years later that I understood her comment. We might not have liked the lives we had but, when you are programmed to accept whatever is dished out to you and that is all you know, it is hard to expect or demand more.

I was eighteen years old when I gave birth to my first child. Jacinda Deidre Mack was born on January 29, 1974, and she changed my life. "Jacinda" means beautiful, and that was what she was to me. Before I had Jacinda, there really was no one to help me because social problems affected everyone in my family and in the community. They couldn't help themselves and certainly not me. The answer to everything back then was, "Don't be a baby. Be tough." I really tried to

My children, Scott, Jacinda, and Tony Mack, 1995 or so

live that way, but sometimes life overwhelmed me. That all changed with the birth of Jacinda.

It seems funny now but, when I was pregnant, I wondered how I would look after a baby. I was the baby of my family at Deep Creek. I had not been around my younger brothers and sisters when they were babies. I had not been around any other babies, so I had no experience whatsoever in this department. Once Jacinda was born and she was placed in my arms, my maternal instincts kicked in, and I knew I would be able to look after her. Not once, even in the toughest times to follow, did I ever seriously think of suicide again. In fact, I was scared something would happen to me, and I worried about who would look after my babies.

When I was still in the hospital with Jacinda, the nurse came to me with a pen and some papers for me to sign. I asked her what they were, and she said, "Adoption papers." I thought they were going to make me sign the papers. I panicked and got very upset. Only then did she back away, "Okay, okay. We just thought you might want to give the baby up." *At no time* had I indicated to anyone that I was thinking of giving up my baby. It makes me wonder how many other Aboriginal girls lost their babies this way.

My second child, Scott Mack, was born May 13, 1975. My sister Dolly had given birth to her daughter Michelle a week before, on May 5, and my sister Teena had given birth to her daughter, Marnie, a few days after that on May 10. We had a good laugh when the nurse asked us if we had all been at the same party. Thankfully, no one came with adoption papers that time.

After Scott, I did not plan to have any more kids. I had a girl and a boy, and I was happy with my little family. Seven years later, however, on June 3, 1982, Tony Mack Jr. was born to my sister Teena and Dayton's nephew, Tony Mack Sr. Teena and Tony Sr. were not together, but Tony flew in from a logging camp right away to be with his son. Dayton and I were supposed to look after Tony Jr. only for a weekend because Tony Sr. had to return to work and couldn't bring his son to a logging camp. After having Tony Jr. for a weekend, a friend who was watching me holding him told me, "You're not giving him back are you?" He was right. I fell in love with Tony as soon as I held him in my arms. Scott and Jacinda were so happy to have Tony as part of our family. Dayton and I legally adopted him.

My life centred on my children and their activities. People would comment on the fact that I always had my kids with me. I truly enjoyed their company. The kids and I made up our family. Even though their dad was around, he was never really around. His other personal interests, wine, women, and song came before us. Thankfully, I did not have to worry about losing my kids to the residential school. They became part of the first generation in our community to attend the public schools from kindergarten on through to high school.

Until 1976, I was content just to stay on the reserve. I looked after my children, but was unhappy in my marriage. I cried a lot but would not let anyone see me cry, not even my kids. I waited until they were asleep before I allowed myself to feel the pain. My sister Dolly later told me that this is probably what helped me get through the years. At least when I was looking after my kids, I was providing myself relief in some form. I believe she is right.

In 1976, Alan Haig-Brown and others started the teacher's aide program in the Williams Lake school district. They wanted Aboriginal teacher's aides in the schools to work with Aboriginal students. Lloyd Sellars, who was a band councillor at the time, gave Alan my name as a possible candidate for the teacher's aide job at Wildwood Elementary School. Alan came to see me at Soda Creek.

I was not too pleased to find this White man standing on my doorstep wanting to talk to me. I didn't want him to come in my house, so we went a short distance and sat on the wooden fence that circled the church. It was a beautiful day. There was a light breeze blowing to keep us cool in the hot sun. Alan explained the program to me and told me that Lloyd thought I would be a good person to work at the school. My first reaction was, "Oh my God, no!" The thought of me walking into a school and working with White teachers terrified me. Alan continued to talk to me about the benefits of the project. I kept telling him that I wasn't interested in working at the school. He would change the subject for a bit and then ease back into the topic of working at the school. He would not accept no for an answer. Finally, I told Alan that I would give it a try. I am sure I agreed just to get rid of him but, once I said yes, I felt I had to follow through.

It was not my first job. I had worked on "make work" projects that were popular in Aboriginal communities at the time. They were supposed to be "training jobs," but there was no training and the projects were of no real benefit to the community. I think they were just projects that someone in some office somewhere decided would be a good idea and would make it look like they were doing something for the Indians. My first job was peeling logs for a community building that never did get built. The first couple of days I, along with about ten other crew members, including my brother Ray and my uncle Johnny, showed up faithfully each morning and stayed until quitting time. One day, I showed up and no one else came to work. I found out that they were all on a drunk. I worked by myself peeling logs. That payday, everyone came to work.

I gave Ray and Johnny heck for not working every day because their paycheque would be pretty small. They didn't say anything and just smiled at each other. I realized why when the paycheques came. Despite the fact that I was the only one who had earned every cent, the whole crew got a full paycheque! My brother Ray and my uncle Johnny had a good laugh at me. They had worked on these projects before and they knew the score. The work project went for a few more weeks and ended before any structure was even started. The logs were hauled away by individual members for use as firewood or something. The next project found us peeling logs to build "another" community building. Despite the fact that I knew I would get a full paycheque even if I worked only for a few days, I continued to work every day. It bothered me at first that I was the only one earning the wages, but I soon got over it. At least Gram got some money from Ray's and Johnny's wages.

I showed up for the first day of school at Wildwood Elementary in September 1976. The principal and his secretary were understandably very busy on that first day. I told the principal who I was, and he stared blankly back at me. He had no idea that I was going to be at the school that day; in fact, he seemed a bit irritated and told me to come back the next day. I went back the next day, and the principal had obviously talked to Alan or someone about my role at the school and he welcomed me more graciously. During my first week helping at the school, I ran into a cousin whose kids were attending and, when she asked what I was doing there, I told her I was working there. She said to me, "Are you the new janitor?" Even though I had no reason to be offended, I was. I had no formal education to allow me to work in the school and, certainly, the only position I may have qualified for at the time was the janitor position. During the year, though, I and other Aboriginal teacher's aides got some training through the school district so we knew how to work with the students.

I had a very hard time the first few months at the school. There were many, many times I just wanted to walk out and never look back. I was uncomfortable going into the teacher's lounge and tried to avoid it as much as possible. I knew the teachers did not have a meaningful role for me because I did not have the training they thought I should. I felt out of place even though a couple of the teachers did try to make good use of my time. I expected to be working with the kids on a daily basis, but my responsibilities fell mainly to making photocopies and putting books away in the library. I did work with a few kids, but they were few and far between. I was not invited to attend staff meetings, but that was a relief to me. Although I was still suffering from the degrading effects of the ridicule I had endured at residential school, I knew my job was intended to be more than just photocopying. At last, I complained to Alan and the woman who worked with him; I didn't have the nerve to complain directly to the principal. Alan's assistant came out and met with the principal a couple of times, but things did not change. After a year and a half, I felt I could no longer work at the school and signed up for an eight-month bookkeeping course at the college in Williams Lake.

That little stint at Wildwood gave me the confidence to venture farther from the reserve. I started to see that I was capable of doing more. I have always been grateful to Alan for not simply taking my no for an answer. Who knows how long I would have stayed on the reserve before I took that first step outside. Maybe, like too many of our people, I would still be there. The reserve, with all its dysfunction, still serves as the safest place in the world for some.

Life on the reserve was safe in some ways but not in others. Drinking and driving created a level of social chaos. My uncle Ernie was always out working and guiding until a car accident disabled him. I remember him coming back from his first attempt at guiding after the accident and crying to Gram that he wasn't the same man he used to be. He couldn't do what he had always done before. Later, Ernie would dictate letters and get me to send them to women and I realized what a lonely man he was. The only person he could really count on was Gram. He always told Gram that he hoped he would die before her because he didn't know what would happen to him if he were left to fend for himself. He got his wish. In his late forties, Ernie went off one night to Williams Lake. The next morning, my grandmother was home alone and heard the dog barking outside. She wondered what he was barking at and finally decided to check. Gram found her son lying in the snow about a hundred yards from our house. She touched his cheek to see if he was alive only to find he was frozen solid. Somehow she made it the half mile to her sister Annie's house and collapsed in her arms.

Many of our people have been killed in motor-vehicle accidents since the 1970s, when cars became common on reserves. Many of our communities are in remote areas, so driving and speeding on poorly maintained roads while drinking not only raises the chances of getting into an accident but also means that medical care for injuries sustained in an accident is rarely immediately available, to put it mildly. I have been involved in a number of car accidents, but usually I was not driving. The one accident in which I was driving, I am grateful to say that no one was hurt. All that changed on May 28, 1978. I had a visitor at my home in Soda Creek, and this woman took great pleasure in telling me about the many infidelities of my husband at the time. I should have been used to it by now, but it still was like a dagger in my heart when I heard those stories. It always made me feel inadequate; I assumed he went with other women because I could not keep him happy. I assumed the problem was with me and I did not realize that he was dealing with feelings of inadequacy of his own.

On the night in question, Dayton was away working in a logging camp, so I decided to drown my sorrows and go out. I left my kids with Mom, and my sisters, Teena and Jean, and I went to town. At the Lakeview Hotel, we ran into my uncle Johnny. We had a few beers and then decided to go to the dance at Sugar Cane. My uncle Johnny jumped in with us. I was driving. When we got to Sugar Cane, the dance had not yet started, so we thought we would go for a drive around the Mission road and back on the highway, a distance of about fifteen miles. By then the dance should have started, we thought. It was pouring rain and the road was slippery in places where there was no gravel, just mud. On the other side of the Mission, as we drove towards a very sharp corner, the truck did not follow the turn when I cranked the wheel. I could feel I had no control of the wheels. We were sliding off the road in the mud. Teena said, "We're going over!" and we rolled three or four times down the steep embankment. When the truck stopped rolling, we were all okay except my uncle Johnny. He was pinned under the truck, still alive but hollering at us to get the truck off him. The only way to get the truck off would be to roll it farther down the hill and, if we did that, he would be crushed because his body was at the lower end of the hill and the truck would have to roll on top of him. The three of us tried to lift the truck uphill, but we couldn't budge it. Johnny kept hollering to get the truck off him. Finally, Teena ran back to the Mission to get help. Jean and I stayed with Johnny. He was getting quieter, and it seemed to be taking Teena a long time to come back. I told Jean I was going to see what had happened to Teena. As I went running down the road, I met Teena on her way back. She had the maintenance person from the Mission with her. It took her so long because she had a hard time finding anyone. We turned around and were going back to the truck to try to get Johnny out from under it when we met Jean. She was pretty shaken up and said, "Johnny's dead." I don't remember much after that. The police came, and I was in the back of the car for a while. It was still pouring rain. I was crying hard, and thinking about Gram. Ernie was gone, we had just buried Ray five months before from complications in hospital, and Leonard had gone fishing out at Farewell Canyon while he was drinking and probably fell in the river through the night. No trace of his body was ever found. Johnny would be her eighth child to die before her. My mom was the only child Gram had left.

I can't describe the intense, intense turmoil I was in. The cop asked me if he should get someone to go to Deep Creek and tell Gram. I said, no, I would do it. I didn't know how I was going to do it, but I knew it had to be me who told Gram. The cop phoned Dolly's husband, Chris Wycotte, to come and get us, and Chris picked us up and took us to Sugar Cane. In our world then, booze was the solution for times like this. I was given a beer, and I did not turn it down, but alcohol could not ease my pain that night. Early the next morning, I woke up and Chris drove my sister Jean and me to Deep Creek. Right away Gram knew something was wrong. I told her what happened and told her I was driving. I don't know how I got through it, but I did. Gram, of course, was shattered. She started to cry and went to her room. I went into the back room and broke down. I did not know how I could live with myself after that. I can't even begin to describe the pain I was in. A short while later, Gram came. She put her arm around my shoulder, and I started to cry even more because I didn't think I deserved the sympathy she was offering.

Gram helped me get through the next few days making funeral arrangements. Of course, she was devastated about her son, but she loved me as well. It amazed me that she could put her intense pain aside to *help me* get through the next few days and weeks. She never chastised me for my involvement in the death of her son. We never talked about the accident once I had told her what happened.

Something else happened that helped me get through the days after the funeral. I was supposed to go into the police station the next day after the accident to make a statement. I didn't go in for a couple of days because I just couldn't deal with reliving the accident so soon. I knew I had to go to the police station so, just before the funeral, Jean and I went to make our statements. I did not want to have to deal with it after the funeral. I knew it was going to be hard enough to get through the funeral. We were sitting in the police station in the waiting area, and Jean was reading a magazine beside me. There was only one cop in the office. No one else was around. I heard someone, almost inaudibly, call my name, "Bevie." I looked at Jean, but she was engrossed in the magazine. I looked at the cop, but he was way at the other end of the office and was not paying any attention to us. Suddenly, I felt a kind of, for lack of a better description, wind go through me, and I *felt*, not heard, someone say, "It's okay." It was my uncle Johnny, telling me that he was all right. I was having a hard time functioning because the guilt and the pain were crippling me. It was just too much to handle until Uncle Johnny came and eased my guilt. I still had nightmares about the accident for years after. I woke up many nights in a cold sweat just as Teena was saying, "We're going over!" I did not imagine the visit from Johnny's spirit. I believe that Johnny knew I needed to be relieved of some of the guilt so I could look after Gram. I know he cared for me as well and, if he was in a good place, he would want me to know that. There was a coroner's inquest into the accident. I was charged with driving too fast for road conditions. Based on evidence from the scene of the accident, the RCMP estimated my speed to be twenty-five miles per hour. After the accident, all the people who I had grown up with at Deep Creek were gone. Xp'e7e, Leonard, Ernie, Ray, Johnny, and Bobby were gone. So we moved to Deep Creek to look after Gram.

Gram was happy that we moved in because she worried about being alone. Mike was living here and there, finding part-time work when he could but he was rarely home. After the accident with Johnny, I was glad to be back in the security of Gram's house at Deep Creek. Gram did not allow parties in her house, so Dayton and his friends had to find somewhere else to party. It was quiet. The kids and I could settle down to having a real home without constantly having to worry about what party crowd was going to come in the middle of the night after the bars closed.

After I finished my bookkeeping course, I went to work for my community. I made five hundred dollars per month for bookkeeping services, and I thought I was making a million bucks. It was the first "big" money I had earned. I stayed in that job for five years and got so bored with it, I decided I needed to do something else. It was my dream to attend university but, at that time, it would mean a move to Vancouver. I couldn't do that to Gram. The least disruptive option I had for my family was to move to Kamloops, a three-hour drive away. Cariboo College offered more programs in Kamloops than in Williams Lake. I wanted to go into a recreation or travel agency program, but the powers that be at the Department of Indian Affairs decided that was not a good choice for me. They "encouraged" me to go into a business administration diploma program. I didn't have the nerve at the time to tell them that the choice had to be mine, so I agreed to go into the program they chose.

I had gotten my high-school equivalency once I knew I wanted to go to college but to get into the business administration program I also had to have Algebra 11. The deadline for applying was three weeks away. I was determined to get into college that year and signed up for Algebra 11 that same afternoon. I completed it successfully within the three-week deadline with a final mark of A plus, sent off my application, and held my breath for a reply. To my relief, I was accepted into the program but I then had to tell Dayton that I wanted to move to Kamloops. I did not know how to do this because I was sure he would not allow it. Even worse, I was afraid he might get violent with me. Even though by this time I had managed to get out from under his control a bit, I was still scared of him. One afternoon, he was working on some machinery in the field in front of our house. I sucked in my breath and went to talk to him. Nervously, I told him of my plans and was amazed at his reaction. After hearing me out, he didn't object to my moving. I was ecstatic. I am sure I floated for the rest of the day, and it was full speed ahead with my plans to move.

In the fall of 1984, my three kids, Gram, and I all moved to Kamloops. Gram was eighty-eight by then, and it was the first time she had been out of Deep Creek since she married seventy years earlier. Gram didn't like Kamloops because there was nowhere for her to exercise, so she rarely left the apartment. She had chopped wood and gone for daily walks around Deep Creek for exercise. It was during our stay in Kamloops that she started to have mobility problems. She could still walk around, but there was a noticeable slowness in her movements that was not evident before we left Deep Creek. In my first semester at Kamloops, I did not realize I could take fewer courses than were listed in the program. I signed up for the full six courses and ended up doing homework before the kids got up in the morning, during Scott's hockey practice, during Jacinda's gymnastics practice, while I was cooking supper, after the kids went to bed, and any time in between I could fit in a bit of studying. I passed all my courses, and the lowest grade I received was a B minus. Gram attributed my doing so well to the "White" side of me. I was mad at her for saying that. The semesters after that only required five courses each, so the rest was easy. At the end of two years, in 1986, I received a certificate from my community that hangs on my wall today. It states that I am the first post-secondary graduate in our community. I never did get a diploma from Cariboo College because, if I applied to graduate, it would cost thirty-five dollars, and I did not have that amount of money to spare.

During one of my high-school years, I remember skipping class and sitting in the Ranch Café with some of my friends. In came Ernie Phillip, a Secwepemc dancer, in full regalia. He had been invited to a school to give a presentation and then came downtown. I don't know if he didn't have time to change or whether leaving his regalia on was intentional. He walked into the restaurant with some Native people from our area, stood and looked around, and then looked straight at the group of us Native kids sitting there. He gave us a big smile and did a little dance to make his regalia jingle. All of a sudden I could feel a surge of pride swell in me. This was the first time I remember something so obviously Aboriginal affecting me this way. I was still brainwashed into thinking that being Native was not anything to be proud of. Usually, anything that was identified as "Indian" was negative but, for at least that afternoon, I was so proud of my Aboriginal heritage. I was also proud that Ernie Phillip acknowledged our table with his smile and dance. It was the first time I had seen someone in full Aboriginal regalia, and it would be years before I saw anyone else dressed so regally. Until 1951, Aboriginal people could wear their regalia and dance only with the permission of the Department of Indian Affairs and only at special events such as stampedes or for dignitaries from other countries. Other than that, it was against the law for Aboriginal people to practise their cultures. So when I was in my teens, the powwows and gatherings that are so popular in Aboriginal communities now were non-existent in our area.

When I was twenty-eight years old and living in Kamloops, I discovered self-help books. I was in a laundromat and decided to go next door to a used bookstore to kill time while waiting for my clothes to dry. I was leafing through books and came across a book called *Discovering the Power of Positive Thinking* by Norman Vincent Peale. I paid twenty-five cents for the book, started reading it, and couldn't put it down. I must have read it a few times just to digest what Peale was saying. Before that, I had not even heard of positive or negative thinking. For me, finding that book was like discovering a gold mine. After that, I bought a few more books and found more in the library.

I started to understand myself and, later, to understand the actions of my family. I did some of the exercises in the books and tried to change the way I thought and acted. It was not easy. Even though I would be aware of things I needed to change and started to see the brainwashing that I had been put through, the change did not come overnight. I had to work consciously on changing my behaviour on a daily basis. When I was scared to do something, I would always tell myself, "You can't let them win. You can't let them win!"

Over the years, the bitterness I felt for some of my family melted away. I was beginning to understand, finally, that all of the social ills in Aboriginal communities could be traced to the destruction of our culture and to the non-Aboriginal institutions that forced their racist policies on us. I cried enough tears to fill a swimming pool during the time I was going through those books. I cried for the suffering of my family. I cried for the inability of our communities to deal with things in a positive manner. I cried for the hurts we kept inflicting upon ourselves. I cried for the hurts we kept inflicting on those closest to us. I cried for the pain that we endured without realizing there was something we could do about it. I cried for the hopelessness that many of my family members lived and eventually died with. I cried for Aboriginal people in general.

I regret that I did not discover those books before I had my children. I cringe when I think of some of the things I did to my kids raising them "Mission style." I did not strap them with a conveyor belt, but I spanked them with my hand and used words that I now realize hurt them. I also expected them to act like adults when they were just kids. "Quit being a baby!" I would tell them. My daughter remembers how she was really upset about something as a young girl and my response to her stress was telling her that she needed to learn how to control her feelings. I meant that she needed to learn how to show no emotion! How I wish I could turn back the years and offer my children the emotional support they needed when they were hurting. Instead, I expected them to do like me, suck it up, accept it, and show no emotion.

Something else I deeply regret is making my children behave "well" in front of White people. I didn't want the White people judging my children, so I tried to make them into perfect little beings while they were in the presence of White people. If they did not behave, they suffered the wrath of my anger. Of course, I did not put that pressure on my kids in the company of Aboriginal people. Over the years, I saw Aboriginal parents forcing the same expectations on their kids, and I knew what they were thinking.

After examining every aspect of my life, I have even gotten over the extremely bitter feelings towards my former husband. Dayton fell into the Fraser River in August 2005, and his body was never found. The Fraser River is a powerful river that does not easily give up its victims. About a year before he died, Dayton asked me to do his last will and testament and he also asked me to be his executor. I agreed, and after he died, I went to collect his papers and among them I found a short journal that he had written about his life. It made me cry to read it. His parents had gone to residential schools, and he talked about being a little boy and some of the things that hurt him over his life. He remembered getting a black eye from his dad when he was trying to protect his mom from a beating. The next day, after his dad sobered up, he took Dayton out for an ice cream to try to make up for the black eye. Dayton also talked about the pain that he felt when I left him but said he couldn't blame me for leaving. I now realize, from the brief glimpses into his childhood that he shared while we were together, that he was in turmoil as well. He dealt with it the same way most dysfunctional men deal with it. He tried to assert control over his life with force. It was not the right way, but too many of us have not learned to deal with our dysfunctional behaviour.

In the last two years of his life, Dayton made real efforts to connect with Jacinda, Scott, and Tony. He was trying to be the father they had so desperately wanted as children. The night before he fell in the river, all three of them visited with him at his home. The connection was working, and I am glad he had that time with them before he left. I never had any doubt that Dayton loved his children. Like too many Aboriginal parents, he did not know how to show it.

My grandson Orden and me down by the Fraser River, circa 2002. I have spent many
days and nights at this exact fishing spot

CHAPTER 12

Becoming
a Leader

While I was still in Kamloops, I got word from some of the people in my community that they wanted me to run for chief in the next election. I was very flattered and did not hesitate to do so. I had run once before, in the 1970s when I was in my early twenties, and thank goodness I did not get in; I was in no way ready for the job and would have made a terrible chief. When I moved back from Kamloops in June 1986, though, I applied for and got the position of administrator for my community. That following April, I ran for chief and at the age of thirty-one was successfully elected. After the election, I ran into a woman from a neighbouring community who had heard that I won the election at Soda Creek. She laughingly told me, "You *do* know that you have to speak in front of people, don't you?" My shyness was legendary, I suppose, but I tried to rise to the occasion. During my first years as chief, I was invited to speak at a gathering at Alkali Lake. I was petrified, but I thought, "Well, it comes with the job," so I agreed. When it was my turn to speak, Dave Belleau introduced me, gave me the mic, and then stepped a few paces away from me. I was shaking so badly I am sure Dave felt the vibration of my knees knocking together through the floorboards of the stage.

Not only did I have to get over my stage fright but, during my first term as chief, I also had a lot to learn. I was politically unaware and really should have had a lot more training for such an important position. With training I might have been more effective but, like so many chiefs across the country, I did my best with what I had.

During the six years that I served as chief, two major events happened. First, our tribal council started to examine, in detail, the issue of the residential schools and, second, the three tribes in our area were successful in getting a Cariboo-Chilcotin Justice Inquiry. The purpose of the inquiry was to investigate and report on the relationship between Cariboo-Chilcotin people and the justice system of the province of British Columbia.

Growing up at Deep Creek, it was nothing unusual for my brothers and uncles to all of a sudden jump up and bolt out the back door into the bush or quickly run upstairs. We had a long driveway and could see any car coming long before it got to our house. Not many cars came down our driveway, so the noise of a car coming was picked up right away. If it was an RCMP vehicle, my brothers and uncles disappeared. It's not that they were criminals. They were peaceful people, yet every one of them, except for Gram, had a criminal record. Most had been in jail only for drinking in a public place, but their experiences with the RCMP were always so negative that they disappeared whenever a cop came around. I learned at an early age that the RCMP were not friends of the Native people and, if I were ever in trouble, they would be the last people I would go to for help.

On more than a few occasions, I saw my uncles and brothers come back from Williams Lake with bruises they said were from the cops. I heard about other members in our community being beaten as well. My uncles, brothers, and grandparents did not question whether the RCMP had the right to do that. It was normal to find out that community members were serving time in jail. The funny thing was that no one ever asked, "What crime did he or she commit?" Guilt or innocence was irrelevant because, if an Indian was accused of a crime, they pleaded guilty just like at the Mission. The residential schools taught us to take our punishment even if we were innocent. The schools taught us that we had no rights and that trying to complain or reveal the truth only made things worse. We learned not to complain. We learned that no one cared whether we were innocent or guilty. We learned that we were totally at the mercy of White authority. So it was easy for me to accept my uncles and brothers coming home with black eyes and bruises that were sometimes inflicted by an RCMP officer. The frustration of being treated as an inferior sometimes couldn't be suppressed, and all the anger and frustration that they were feeling boiled out in violence. That only gave the RCMP another excuse to use force against them.

When the opportunity for a justice inquiry came along in 1993, I felt that we had even more of a chance to change things. I knew the judicial system was still abusing Aboriginal people, maybe not to the same extent as twenty years earlier but nevertheless abuse was still happening. I had very high hopes that an inquiry would bring injustice out into the open and finally things could change. Others were not so certain. My brother-in-law, who had many encounters with the RCMP, even laughed at me and accused me of having my head in the clouds for thinking real change could happen. I was told that thirty or more Native communities had already conducted inquiries, and all the reports that resulted were gathering dust on some basement shelf. I wasn't discouraged. Even if it were true, I was still sure we could change things in the Cariboo-Chilcotin.

Our stories would be heard as part of an inquiry that Joan Gentles, a Tsilhqot'in (Chilcotin), had initiated. She wanted an inquiry for her people and she pushed for inclusion of the Carrier and Secwepemc people who live in the area. When we heard that there would be an inquiry, we had just a few weeks to prepare our people for it. We have fifteen Aboriginal communities, with people from three nations: southern Carrier, Chilcotin, and northern Secwepemc. Representatives from the three nations were chosen: Joan Gentles for the Chilcotin people, Mary William for the Carrier, and me for the Secwepemc. We began the process of trying to determine how to reach all our people in such a short time.

We hired a couple of lawyers and almost immediately had to dismiss them. They treated us as children who couldn't think for themselves and made statements on our behalf without our approval. So we hired new lawyers to represent us – Bryan Williams, who later became chief justice of the Supreme Court of British Columbia; Glen W. Bell; and Don Sorochan, who later would become my principal when I articled at the law firm of Miller Thomson LLP.

Judge Anthony Sarich was put in charge of the justice inquiry. Our first meeting with Judge Sarich and representatives for the RCMP began with introductions. As usual, the Native people gathered at one end of the room, and the lawyers and all the other non-Natives were at the other end. Everyone was asked to introduce themselves and, as soon as the White people had finished introducing themselves, the meeting was called to order. Joan Gentles spoke up and said, "Excuse me! We are here too, and we would like to introduce ourselves." It was then that I realized that we were seen, once again, as minor players in this game. Even though the justice inquiry was supposed to be conducted on our behalf, we weren't seen as important or even relevant, even though we were sitting in the same room. That was the first insult to us. Then the RCMP went to the Supreme Court of British Columbia to try to block any testimony by Aboriginal people. They were unsuccessful, but the whole story received national attention.

Dozens of Native people lined up to tell their stories during the justice inquiry. All of the testimony was on a voluntary basis, and people seemed willing to tell their story to the lawyers who represented us. Everyone knew of someone else who should be interviewed. But when the time came for them to testify at the inquiry, they saw all the lawyers for the RCMP sitting around their table and felt intimidated. Many decided they didn't need to tell their story, and they fell away left and right. Stacking the table with lawyers was a deliberate intimidation tactic on the part of the RCMP. Another tactic was for some lawyers to interview the witnesses as if they were on trial. Then the RCMP brought in a special prosecutor, Jimmy someone or other, who was known to be tough. I realized things weren't looking good when Bryan Williams, who knew the special prosecutor's work, turned to his co-counsel and said, "They're bringing in Jimmy!"

We were up against a symbol that many Canadians hold in the highest regard. The saying that Mounties "always get their man" is a household expression. People from Williams Lake testified to all the good work that was being done in our communities. Staff sergeants gave glowing reports about the excellent working relationship between the RCMP and the Aboriginal communities. Representatives from other agencies would go on for hours about the things they were doing to improve justice for Native people. Much of what they said was news to us. I was the chief of my community at the time, and these initiatives were unknown to me. As leader of the community, I should have known about the work they were doing or planning on doing. How could we not have been aware of it?

During the justice inquiry, someone handed us a poem that one of the lawyers for the RCMP had written and circulated on the other side as a big joke against us. We were outraged at its racist attitude and then were further insulted when our lawyers advised us to "chalk it up to ignorance" and ignore it. I couldn't understand how they could suggest that to us. Ignorance was the reason we were holding this justice inquiry. Aboriginal people refused to ignore it in the same way that we did not want to ignore all past injustices against us. We chose to deal with the matter up front, and a meeting was set up at Toosey, one of the Chilcotin communities. The author of the poem, of course, did not show up. The justice inquiry was nothing but a big joke to the people who represented the RCMP and other judicial officials. Here is the poem that RCMP officer wrote:

THE INQUIRY BLUES / EPIC ? All dat I listen, to tales of woe.
That happened many years ago. Tales of blood, and beer of course.
Of men in red and excessive force. Of calls not made, to those who wait.
For the RCMP to investigate. Wrapped in sorrow, all alone.
It finally dawns that she has no phone. The innocent man, which the
system wronged.
Now has a place to sing his song. Of being pled guilty, to the charge as laid.
By "pale-faced" lawyers from legal aid. The Boitanio Mall, must share
the shame.
They victimize the poor and lame. Who drink a case of beer, and say.
I remember well when I drink that way. The province too, should feel
remorse.
For not providing a form of course. To put your licence, in your friend's
name.
So when you're caught you don't get blamed.

....

We're all confused, it's just not clear.
Perhaps I'll drink a case of beer. To clarify my train of thought.
Of all the harm the white man wrought.

....

Valentine's Day, we come back here.
To chat with Tony, drink some beer. So we listen to what Tony's seen.
And wonder where the hell he's been. We thought the man, had cooked
his goose.
When Williams took him from the noose. And the "Bull" is now all puffed
with pride.
She's got a bigger horse to ride.

....

We head for Toosey, the very next day.
But the natives just don't want to play. Jimmy's taken all their fun.
And has the warriors on the run. So "Gentle Joan", all full of pain.
Climbs on board old Tony's train. She says her folks aren't treated right.
So Joan and Jimmy smoke the pipe. Now we wait, with baited [sic] breath.

New incidents of sudden death. Of bighorn sheep, and painted cars.
Of natives drinking in the bars. Of high speed chases, to the chief.
And mothers dealing with their grief. Burning fires, where children die.
We watch young Setah (Marshall) lie.

....

The Inquiry Blues, are a state of mind.
Of mass confusion that we find. Does not get better, as we go on.
And so I write this little song.

....

CHORUS
"Confused we are, confused we be. Is everyone confused as me?"

The recommendations that came out of the justice inquiry were
disappointing, to say the least. The inquiry was unable to get at the
heart of the problem because of many barriers put up by lawyers
for the RCMP and because of the intimidation tactics they used on
our people. Judge Sarich, to his credit, made an effort to control the
lawyers but, in the end, the result was not what we had envisioned.

So now the *Report on the Cariboo-Chilcotin Justice Inquiry* sits on
the shelf gathering dust. Have things improved? I guess that depends
on who you talk to. Some say things have improved, some say there has
been no change, and some say things have gotten worse. Not too long
after the justice inquiry, an Aboriginal man died in jail in Williams
Lake. There was another inquiry into it, and investigators determined
that it had been a homicide but couldn't say who was responsible.

While I was chief of the Soda Creek Band, the other major event
that happened is that our tribal council started to look at the effects
of residential schools on our people. Eventually we held the First
National Conference on Residential Schools in Vancouver in June
1991, and I was asked to give the opening remarks. I started to prepare
what I wanted to say. I had never talked about the schools in public
before, and I found that I couldn't get through what I wanted to say

without breaking down. I spoke to a counsellor who was working in our community at the time. I told her I was having problems just getting through the presentation in private rehearsal and that I was scared I would not be able to go through with it in front of all those people. After some discussion she said to me, "People who have not been to the schools may think you are weak if you break down during your speech." That remark clinched it for me. I did the presentation without a hitch, putting in enough emotion to make it effective but not allowing myself to break down. My thought was, "Like hell if I am going to allow them to judge me again." I was able to bluntly say what I needed to say without sidestepping the issues about residential schools. My presentation that day was eventually printed in a number of books and people in college classes over the years told me they used the material I had written.

During our examination of the residential schools, a number of healing workshops were brought into our area. It was during one of these workshops that I realized how lucky I was to have been raised at Gram's place. We were doing a visualization exercise and were told to take ourselves back to the home where we were raised. We were all lying on the floor with our eyes closed. We had to use all our senses. What did we see while we were at our house? What smells were coming from the house? What sounds were coming from the house, and how did they make us feel? It was an enjoyable exercise for me because I went back to a summer day outside my grandparents' house. When it was too hot, I would sometimes lie in the tall grass beside the house and look at the clouds. I was always barefoot. Inside I heard Gram and my uncles gently talking. I could smell Gram's homemade bread fresh out of the oven, and I felt content.

My enjoyment of going back in these memories was broken by the sound of people crying around me. One man cried so loudly I wanted them to shut him up because his sorrow was ruining my good memories. Later, when we sat around and discussed the experience, the stories that others told about their childhood memories shocked me. The man whose crying was so loud said that when he visualized being outside his parents' house, he smelled home brew coming from the house, heard people fighting and things breaking, and felt fear and agony. Most of the people in the group had memories of their childhoods that involved drinking and negative feelings.

For the most part, Gram had protected me from that.

Also during my term as chief, word came that the Oblate priests were selling the St. Joseph's Mission land and buildings. We were told that we could retrieve pictures and other personal stuff that had been collected there over the years. Like others, I went over to see if there were any pictures I might want. Some of my group took a few pictures of their grandmothers and others that hung on the wall. After we left, I heard that former students from the school came from the surrounding reserves – some travelled more than a hundred miles – and tore that building apart. A group of us went back the next day and I was shocked at the smashed windows, sodden floors, and total destruction of that huge building. It's not that I was shocked that former students would do this. I could understand that. I was shocked at how much damage they were able to do in less than twenty-four hours with no tools or machinery. All the anger and hatred that former students felt towards the Mission was evident in the destruction of that building.

It was during my term as chief that I met Hemas Kla-Lee-Lee-Kla (Chief Bill Wilson), a hereditary chief of the Kwawkgewlth / Musgamagw from Kingcome Inlet and Gilford Island on the B.C. coast. Bill tells everyone that I chased him all over the province before he slowed down long enough for me to catch him.

Bill and I first met in June 1990 when he came up to Williams Lake to speak to a high-school graduating class as chair of the First Nations Congress. During that visit, our communities had a dinner for all the students at the longhouse in Williams Lake. Joan Gentles, who by this time was the education coordinator for School District No. 27, invited Bill to be the keynote speaker for the dinner. After Bill spoke, I noticed that he was standing outside by himself looking very out of place. As one of the local chiefs, I felt I had a duty to make him feel welcome. I went over to talk to him, but the conversation didn't last more than a few sentences. He didn't seem to want to talk, so I left him alone. I later saw him staring at me through the crowd. In September of that same year, when we were attending a political meeting in Vancouver, I ended up in the Chateau Granville lounge with a group of co-workers. Bill came over and we started talking. Until I started to go to provincial meetings, I had only a vague idea of who he was. I had seen news clips of him with other Aboriginal leaders, but that was about the extent of my exposure to the Aboriginal political world. My little world centred mostly on what was happening in my community. I was, for the most part, oblivious to the fact that there was a whole movement by Aboriginal people across Canada to change the conditions in our communities.

In the Chateau that evening, Bill told me a bit about himself, including the fact that he was married. He then said, thankfully not in the same breath, that he wanted to have some sort of a relationship with me. I told him that he should look me up when he was divorced. We went our separate ways that night. When I saw him at other Aboriginal meetings, he let me know that he was still interested. I had never met an Aboriginal person like him. He intimidated me. At a conference in Victoria in 1990, Bill became famous for saying to the White people, "Maybe we should have killed you all." He was referring to the horrendous way Aboriginal people were and, in many cases, still are treated. Bill said what so many other Aboriginal people thought: instead of helping the newcomers, maybe the Aboriginal people should have killed them all.

Bill saw me in the audience at that conference. I should have known he would be going in for the kill from the looks I was getting from him. After the session was over, I left the conference room. I was standing outside talking to some people when Bill came rushing out of the conference room. He was a bit overweight and the short jaunt obviously was somewhat of a strain for him. He looked kind of silly and I had to laugh. He came over, steered me aside from my group, and asked if I would go to supper with him and a couple of his friends. I had already made other plans, but he managed to convince me to have dinner with them. After dinner, we left his friends, went for a long walk around Victoria harbour, and talked. That night, *I* was the one who slowed down long enough for Bill to catch me.

If Bill had left it up to me, we would not have lasted but a few months in our relationship. It was so full of passion but, at the same time, it was stormy. We fought on a regular basis during those first years. There was no physical violence in our relationship, except for the one time early in our relationship that I slapped and punched him as hard as I could. Anger was still a big part of my life, and I was so angry with him that I physically attacked him. My violent reaction stunned him.

Even though I still have problems sometimes dealing with anger, Bill was the one who taught me that there is a better way. If I was upset with him, my automatic reaction was to shut down. He would not let me off the hook and would say, "Let's just deal with it and move on." That was a new concept to me. I was not comfortable with talking about why I was upset, but he would not leave me alone until I told him why. Eventually, I would reluctantly tell him what was bothering me and we would talk about it. Sometimes I still would go storming off but, other times, I would realize I was being silly or we would resolve the conflict.

Bill also taught me to accept compliments gracefully. I was embarrassed when I received one because sincere compliments were something I was not used to. Bill also helped me to take criticism without getting angry. Bill would comment on my dysfunctional actions but would almost immediately say after a criticism, "I love you" or compliment me on something else. That made it easier for me to take criticism and eventually taught me that it was okay to have flaws. I even learned to laugh at myself, something I was unable to do before.

Bill is politically the most brilliant man I have ever met, and I am not alone in that opinion. Supreme Court judges, political scientists, friends, enemies, other leaders, and acquaintances would agree. Whether people love him or hate him, everyone agrees with his brilliance in the political field. He is also unafraid to say the truth about the conditions of Aboriginal people. I have seen him on many occasions take on White politicians and, because of Bill's truthfulness and aggressiveness, they have caved in or at least realized that they are not dealing with just any Indian. They can't push this one around. Nothing makes Bill angrier than someone treating him as an inferior. I have seen him attack and bring down those who feel any superiority over him. Bill has many White friends, and I am amazed at how he talks to them. He has no inhibitions about anything he says to them. He jokes and teases them a lot of times, and sometimes their programmed way of thinking about Aboriginal people allows him to point out their ignorance in a very comical way. Other times, situations present themselves as the perfect opportunity to crack a joke.

Once we were sitting in the Caffé dé Medici, a high-priced Italian restaurant in Vancouver that is considered very classy. The maître d' liked Bill, so we were treated well whenever we went there. This particular time, our food was delivered to the table but we had no cutlery. Bill, in a booming voice loud enough for everyone in the restaurant to hear, said to the maître d', "Can we have some cutlery, please? I know we are Indians but this is ridiculous!" That poor man was so embarrassed, he couldn't get our cutlery to us quick enough. The rest of us at the table all laughed, but the mainly White customers in the restaurant looked very uncomfortable and some even looked angry. I guess we are not supposed to crack these kinds of jokes in a restaurant like that.

Over the years, Bill and I have worked side by side on many projects. I have seen his extraordinary skill to speak and write eloquently.

His ability to analyze instantly even the most complex problems amazes me. The letters he dictates to me are always grammatically perfect; the only corrections are my punctuation marks. He also speaks as well as he writes. He has never used a speech writer. He plans his speeches in his mind, memorizes them, and then only uses an index card to remind him of his main points. On many occasions, I've seen non-Aboriginal groups who were opposed to Aboriginal rights and treaties give him standing ovations after he finished speaking.

I've seen Bill criticized for being a radical or too provocative but sometimes that is what we need to make people listen to what Aboriginal people are saying. There are many things wrong in our communities, and many people don't care about the conditions in which we are forced to live. Bill's extreme self-confidence introduced me to a whole new world. He knows everyone everywhere and, in places where he does not know anyone, there is always someone who knows who he is. I have never seen Bill feel intimidated in any way by anyone or anything. He is always in charge of any situation. I was quite surprised when he admitted to me that he still gets butterflies in his stomach before he makes a speech. You would never know he is the least bit nervous.

Ever since I discovered self-help books, I have worked hard to change the way I see myself and those around me. I try to remember that everyone is just human and, even though we may have different colour skin or we may physically look different, inside we are all basically the same. Bill pulled me into the so-called upper echelons of society and it was only then that I fully grasped that people are all the same. He introduced me to people in all political circles, people I had only seen on TV. I had lunch and chatted with Mila Mulroney when her husband was prime minister. I watched a large group of New Democrat and later Liberal party members get totally wasted at political events. I saw high-ranking lawyers and judges who were intoxicated acting as stupid as any person in my community in the same state. I watched Bill and Jack Webster, a prominent talk-show host in Vancouver who was on at "9:00 a.m. precisely," drink and get silly in the Hotel Vancouver. I sat and watched and realized that these people really were no different than me or any of the people in my community. It was only after hanging around with Bill and watching these "perfect" people that I was no longer intimidated by anyone.

Today, I do not put anyone on a pedestal. I have respect for people and for their achievements, but I also know that if they are down in the dumps or extremely well off, they have had help to get where they are. I have come a long way from the girl who was sure that just by being White meant you were better. Bill provided me with that final push out of my intimidated and oppressed thoughts. Now the only hang-ups I have are the ones that all people have, like speaking in front of a crowd. Even though I have done it on a regular basis, it still is a bit scary.

Bill and me today

CHAPTER 13

Going to University

While I was going to school in Kamloops, I found out that some of my friends were taking courses that were transferrable to universities. I dreamed of going to university but didn't think it would ever happen because of my family and community commitments. The opportunity came in 1993. Our community had our elections for chief and council coming up again in April, and I decided not to run. An incident that happened a few months before made me realize that it was time to step down as chief and do something else.

I was heading into town in my vehicle. Dealing with the Department of Indian Affairs and ignorant White people in general always made me angry, and that day was no exception. I was in a bad mood and passed three young White boys who were hitchhiking. I did not know them and did not stop to pick them up even though I easily had enough room in my vehicle for all of them. I happened to glance in my rear-view mirror as I passed them and saw that one of them had given me the finger. All of a sudden, I felt such intense anger. That little gesture brought back full force all of the hatred I felt towards White people. Even though I probably got the finger for not stopping to pick them up, it brought back all the racist policies that the Department of Indian Affairs had forced on our people. It brought back the inequities of the justice inquiry, and it brought back all of the negative social conditions my people had to endure because of the White ancestors of these three boys.

I turned my vehicle around and drove back past the boys, then pulled a U-turn and steered my vehicle straight towards them. They had to jump off the side of the road to avoid getting run over. I stopped the vehicle, got out, and went over to where they stood, swearing a blue streak at them for giving me the finger. They were big boys, and it never occurred to me that I might be putting myself in danger. Instead, they seemed to be in shock. I screamed at them and all the hatred I felt came pouring out of me. One of the boys started talking back to me and we got into a screaming match. I finally got back in my car and drove away, leaving them standing on the road. I fully expected a visit from the RCMP but no one came looking for me. Maybe the boys were just too surprised to get my licence plate number. That incident helped me realize I was getting way too cynical. My anger at the way my people were forced to live was getting to me.

Over the years, I had watched my protective big brother Mike deteriorate from work in coastal logging camps or planting trees in the Interior to drinking too much and working less and less. Eventually, he became a chronic alcoholic on the streets of Williams Lake. One time, Mike was ordered by the courts to attend a treatment centre in Prince George. He came back looking healthy and said he was glad to no longer wake up with a hangover. I asked him if he was going to quit drinking for good. He said that although he liked being healthy, being sober also allowed him to start thinking about his life – something he didn't like to do. Whenever his mind ran back to earlier events, he wanted a drink so he wouldn't think. It wasn't too long before Mike was drinking again.

Years later, I spotted Mike picking up bottles near a McDonald's restaurant outside Williams Lake. I turned the car around and went to talk to him. We exchanged a few words and I gave him twenty dollars. Just as I was about to leave, Mike said to me, "Don't ever think I don't miss you, Bev." I got all choked up and told him that I missed him too. Of course, we didn't hug or even touch. He just walked away, and in my rear-view mirror, I watched him head towards town. He had stopped picking up bottles because he had enough money to buy his booze for the day.

My heart was broken. I cried off and on all the way through my day. I cried for the young man he once was, the potential he had, the dreams that had been squashed, the dark memories and anger he tried to escape with the use of alcohol and drugs. I cried for the person he had become. My big brother had been reduced to one of society's outcasts – nothing more than a dirty nuisance that needed to be obliterated.

Yes, in some ways Mike had become a threat to society. Over the years, he told me some of the things he had done to other people, and I found it difficult to imagine this protective man harming others. Mike, however, did not get to this place all by himself. Like so many other people, Aboriginal or not, Mike had a lot of help getting where he is today. Mike never told me directly but, based on a few hints he let slip over the years, I suspect that he had been sexually abused at the Mission. He suffered from the same low self-esteem that I had and he quit school in grade nine or ten. I think Mike's life was predetermined before he ever left the Mission. Booze for Mike was an escape that he adopted early in life, and it had him in a full headlock by the time he was in his early twenties. How could he possibly live up to his full potential with all that hurt and pain weighing him down?

The streets of Williams Lake are full of men like Mike. They nickname themselves the "Troopers." All have relatives in the surrounding communities and families who love them. All are human beings no matter how bad they may look. They have funny and interesting stories, and they are loyal to their friends and relatives. Many times, though, I have watched non-Aboriginal people walk by these street people with a look of disdain, dislike, and even sometimes a look bordering on hatred. They quickly condemn the Troopers but simply have no idea of what Aboriginal people have experienced. What do non-Aboriginal people know of the discrimination we have been put through for their benefit? What do they know of the feelings we have for them but do not show?

When Mike first started to live on the streets, he would plan his trips to jail so that he could spend the winters under a warm roof with three square meals a day. He knew what crime to commit, how long it would take to get through the courts, and what sentence he was likely to get. One summer, Mike told me that it was almost time for him to do a break and enter. He knew what time of year to commit a crime so that he would be out by the next spring.

Doing time in jail was not a hardship for many Aboriginal people. My brother Morris spent many years in prison. He said, as did many others, that the residential school was worse than any prison. Morris spent ten years at the Mission, longer than most. He said he would have spent less time there, but he got into trouble with the law and, when given a choice of going to jail or back to the Mission, he chose the Mission because he had never been to jail before. Later, after he did go to jail, Morris remembered his choice and said, "If I knew jail was going to be better than the Mission, I would have gladly gone to jail." It is a sad, sad situation when the prison system is a step up from the residential-school experience.

Oscar Williams from Sugar Cane, like so many of our people, spent a good deal of time in prison. At one court hearing, Oscar was sentenced to nine months in prison. He told the judge, "I can do that standing on my head!" So the judge added another three months, giving Oscar "time to get back on his feet." Oscar went to prison so many times that he learned the justice system and started to defend himself in court. He became quite good at it and was a thorn in the side of the RCMP in Williams Lake. They would manage to convict him of something, and he would appeal the sentence and be back in Williams Lake in no time.

In 1990, at the age of ninety-four, Gram decided to move away from Deep Creek. Although I still lived there with her, Gram found she was alone too much because I travelled a lot in my job as chief and, even when I was home, I was often out of the house with my kids and their many activities. During the winter at Deep Creek, Gram had to go downstairs to put wood in the heater in the basement and that was getting to be too much for her. Gram was still independent. She cooked for herself and still tried to bake bread. At first, she insisted that she stay by herself in her house at Deep Creek. When she began to find it difficult to walk and needed someone to live with her and look after her, we renovated her old house at Soda Creek, which was right next door to Mom, and Mom went over daily to check on her. With Mom's help, my grandmother lived by herself until she was ninety-eight years old. Eventually, Mom got a new house that was up the hill and a long ways away from Gram, so Gram decided to move in with Mom. Mom's taking responsibility for Gram allowed me to take a much-needed break from Aboriginal politics and go to university.

Jacinda and Scott were on their own by this time. Bill encouraged me to fulfill my dream of going to university. I eagerly applied and was accepted into the University of Victoria. Tony, who was still at home with us, moved with Bill and me to Victoria. I was thirty-eight years old and admitted to the university as a mature student.

University opened up a whole new way of thinking for me. Little light bulbs in my brain went off left, right, and centre. The experience was just as liberating as when I had discovered self-help books. My first-year studies in university included psychology, philosophy, political science, and English. It was also recommended that I take a history course, but I didn't want to because I knew that all the history that I had been taught up to then was inaccurate and I had Gram's voice in my head.

Gram always talked about how she did not like what the White people did to the Indians, but she never confronted non-Aboriginals or told them no if they asked for something. I guess her residential school training stayed with her throughout her life too. She told me about Eddie Herd, a White man who lived near the Aboriginal people. Eddie Herd was a poor man when he came to the Williams Lake area. He would regularly go house to house in the Aboriginal community bumming things he needed from the Aboriginal people. Of course, the Aboriginal people always helped him out. When Eddie Herd finally made it on his own and established a productive ranch near Deep Creek, he turned his back on the Aboriginal people who had helped him. Gram said they would be walking down the street in Williams Lake and, when Eddie Herd saw them coming, he would cross the street so he would not have to talk to them. Eddie Herd would not even acknowledge the Native people who had helped him for years. That seemed to be the common theme of interactions between Aboriginal people and newcomers. Gram said, "The Indians saved lots of those White people. They didn't know how to get around in this country; now they think the Indians are no good."

History that I had been taught up until I went to university started with the White man. I knew Aboriginal history began in this country long before that. I tried to fit other courses into my schedule but, in the end, the only one that would work was a history course. Resigning myself to the situation, I decided to suck it up for the first semester, take the history course, and get the three credits I needed for a full-year course. Once I got into class, I was amazed that for the first two weeks we talked about history before everyone else got here – the history of Aboriginal people. Things had definitely changed since the last course I had taken more than twenty years before. I eventually majored in history.

My other courses were all so interesting. I learned about non-Aboriginal politics and their party platforms and policies. I took a couple of courses in international politics and learned how countries interact with one another. I studied Plato and Aristotle and their views of raising children to be the best they could be. That made me think about the upbringing of most Aboriginal children, and the contrast was stark – Aboriginal kids were raised to self-destruct; nothing in our training was geared to help us do our best. In philosophy class, I learned to think critically and to question everything. I even learned to ask, "Is there a God?" I had been so programmed into just accepting the existence of a God who we all will answer to at the end of our lives. Maybe I had not fully embraced the Catholic church's teachings in my life, but I was scared enough to believe they might hold some truth. When I first met Bill and one of our discussions got around to religion he told me, "You know there isn't a God, don't you?" I was sure he was going to be struck down right there and then. The more I read and thought about what I was learning, the more I could see that organized religion was a tool men in power had invented to control people. I thought about the teachings at the Mission and saw the total hypocrisy of their organization. I lost any respect I may have had for organized religion.

In history, I learned that much of the philosophical basis of environmental education stems from the Aboriginal people's relationship with the land. One of my history books said that the Iroquois had a days-long Thanksgiving ceremony in honour of the sun, the wind, the rain, the earth, and everything that grows. The Europeans thought this "pagan" relationship to the land was proof of inferiority. Today, everyone knows the importance of our relationship to the land. Later I realized other courses included the teachings of Aboriginal people. The more research is done, the more we realize that people all over the world enjoy the fruits of Aboriginal contributions without being aware of their origin, from plant-based medicine and world cuisine, to sports and military strategy, to government, language, and architecture and so on and so on. All races have contributed to what we have and learn today.

I went on to get a law degree from the University of British Columbia, articled with Miller Thomson LLP, and went to work for the B.C.

Treaty Commission in Vancouver. I often went back to Soda Creek to visit Gram and the rest of the family, and on one of my visits to Gram, she had cooked a whole meal for me. By age ninety-nine, though, Gram had become very sick and very skinny. I stayed with Mom for four months that summer and nursed Gram while she was sick. I was sure she was going to die, so every day I made her take a few teaspoons of *hooshum* (whipped soapberries, also known as Indian ice cream), and that is all she would eat. Then one day she woke up and declared, "I'm hungry!" Gram recovered fully from then on, but at the age of one hundred, she fell and broke her hip, and we had to move her into Deni House, a care facility. My daughter, my niece Marnie, and I all took turns going into the hospital every day to make sure Gram's needs were being met. Gram's mental abilities were intact until the evening before she died. She then started laboured breathing and we knew the time was soon. We all said our goodbyes to her and told her that we loved her. I leaned and whispered in her ear that if she needed to go, then she should go. She was surrounded by her family when she died about two o'clock in the morning.

I really get angry when non-Aboriginal people become "experts" on Aboriginal people. They come into our territories and gather information for four or five years and they become the experts and our elders like Gram, who have lived the life of a First Nations woman, become mere footnotes. Aboriginal people are the only experts on Aboriginal people. I don't care how many years people go to school to learn about us. Unless they have lived our lives, they are not the experts.

When I first ran for chief of my community, it was not because I saw the whole political picture of how things needed to improve for Aboriginal people. I ran because some of my community members were unhappy with the way a few programs were being administered on our reserve. It was about this time that programs were being transferred from the Department of Indian Affairs to administration by the chief and council in our communities.

In my second two-year term as chief, I started going to a few provincial meetings as part of my duties. It was at these meetings that I received what I call my "Masters in Aboriginal Politics." Only after listening was I able to connect the everyday issues that happened in my community to the bigger political picture. I was amazed at what I heard and the anger I saw at these meetings. People were mad about the way Aboriginal people were being treated, and the feelings expressed were like none I had heard before. I remember at one of these meetings, Bill said, "All the money you get from the government is welfare! Until we rightfully take our place in society and have control of the money that comes from our territories, it is all welfare!" That statement shocked me, but those kinds of statements opened up a new way of thinking.

At one of these meetings, I was on a pay phone when reporters were chasing George Watts, a high-profile Aboriginal leader, for an interview about Meares Island, which his people were trying to protect from logging. He turned around a short distance from me and the message he sent to government and the logging industry through the media left a lasting image in my mind. George was angry and he let them know it. The thing that amazed me most was his ability to speak his mind without inhibition and to articulate his opinion from a position of strength and confidence. George and Bill were not prisoners in their minds like too many of us who attended the schools. There have been many Aboriginal leaders, right from first contact, who have continued to fight for our rights, but many of us were temporarily disabled. Over the years and with my two university degrees – a bachelor of arts with a major in history and minor in political science and a bachelor of law – I have become aware of the bigger issues, not only in my community and in other Aboriginal communities, but also to some degree around the world.

CHAPTER 14

Final Thoughts

I have been told many times that I need to "forgive" in order to move on with my life. I say bull to that. It is not up to me to forgive. Forgiveness is an easy out for those who have inflicted all the pain and suffering on Aboriginal people. Forgiveness and reconciliation too easily absolve us of our responsibility to find solutions to conflicts. Forgiveness allows the perpetrators to get away with not being accountable for their actions. Is this like the Catholic confessional, where even for the most horrendous crimes, one can go to confession, say a few prayers, and get forgiveness in the eyes of God? Is this why the abuses continued? Is that how the abusers in the schools lived with themselves? There can be no forgiveness for evil done in the guise of religion and there can be no forgiveness for racism.

The churches and governments have reduced once-independent Aboriginal nations to beggars in our own lands. While all the harm and damage cannot be repaired, there is much that can change if non-Aboriginals, individuals, and governments abandon the assumption that they know what is best for Aboriginal people. Economies based on renewable, sustainable natural resources must be returned to Aboriginal people, and the sooner we can assume control of our lives, the better it will be for all Canadians. There is a saying that only two things in life are certain: death and taxes. I always remind people that there is one more thing in life that is certain and that is that First Nations people will always be in our territories. We have been here for thousands of years and we will be here for thousands more. We do not have a homeland to which we can return. This is our homeland and we are not going anywhere. Aboriginal people will, of course, make mistakes in governing ourselves just as any nation in the world today makes mistakes. Aboriginal people have to be allowed to make our own mistakes and then, and only then, can people legitimately criticize us. So let's talk about forgiveness only when real dialogue and change take place in Canada.

Thankfully times are changing. For example, we just had an Aboriginal person finish his term as Lieutenant Governor for British Columbia. Steven Point is from the Stó:lō Nation in the Fraser Valley. I think a cartoon that appeared in one of the newspapers after Steven was appointed as lieutenant governor said it all. There was a picture of two men shaking hands. One is obviously a White man in a suit and the other is Steven as the new lieutenant governor. Steven is wearing the uniform required in his role as spokesperson for the Queen. The White guy shaking Steven Point's hand says, "You've come a long way." Steven Point in return says, "So have you." We have come a long way in our relationship with each other, but we still have a long way to go to create a society that will benefit us all. I hope other Canadians who have benefitted from the many riches in this country will support Aboriginal people and our efforts to take our rightful place in society instead of responding to us with the knee-jerk reaction that Aboriginal people get everything for nothing. That simply is not true.

Aboriginal people are still attempting to rebuild badly cracked but not completely broken communities. I hope Aboriginal and non-Aboriginal people look beyond the obvious and try to understand our communities. My nephew Robert Sellars said after reading a draft of this book, "Maybe now I can forgive my dad for some of the things he did." That is the reaction I want for those who are struggling to understand why there is so much hurt in their families. Programming in one's most vulnerable years is extremely difficult to overcome. I think of the cults from which families steal their loved ones back and have them deprogrammed from indoctrination. Aboriginal people too need to deprogram the destructive teachings of the residential schools and non-Aboriginal institutions. Like a computer that cannot run at its full potential if it has viruses, Aboriginal people need to eradicate the destructive viruses so that we can run at our full capacity. Without understanding how destructive the teachings were, we will continue to look at our social issues on a superficial level and continue to blame those closest to us.

At fifty-eight years of age, I now have finally come to a place in my life where I am comfortable with who I am. Moving beyond my experience at St. Joseph's Mission, I feel my "mission" now is to make Aboriginal people realize that it is time we started living again and not just surviving. I think of the nuns and priests at residential school, who replaced my name with a number, and I say it is time for us all to realize that we need to make ourselves "Number One" in our lives. It is time for us to realize that we need to make ourselves a priority and not feel ashamed or reduced by that experience. Someone said that I am a survivor but I believe I am much more than that. I prefer to claim outright victory in this war against the residential-school experience. Even though I sometimes barely survived, I didn't become one of the terrible statistics of Aboriginal people. In the end, I win! Residential school did not manage to beat the Indian out of me and my Aboriginal pride just keeps getting stronger. I look around and I see many more like me. It makes my heart swell and it makes me hopeful for the future of our Aboriginal nations. I win.

Afterword

BY WENDY WICKWIRE

Last spring, the Lytton Band threw a retirement party for Ruby Dunstan. After a feast and a welcome by Chief Janet Webster, community members and chiefs, environmental activists, and others took to the stage with laudatory speeches. I was there with my partner, Michael M'Gonigle, as part of the Stein Valley contingent. In the mid-1980s, we had worked with Ruby, then chief of the Lytton Band, in a battle to "save" the local Stein Valley from logging. The venue for the party was the gymnasium of the new Stein Valley Nlaka'pamux School, an appropriate place given Ruby's roles in both the Stein campaign and the creation of the band school.

The school fosters a new culture of education, but its locus also evokes a dark side of the community's history, a collective history that Ruby Dunstan shares with Bev Sellars. The Stein School stands on the site of St. George's Indian Residential School which, from its founding in 1901 until its closure in 1979, dominated the lives of all Nlaka'pamux families. The school complex occupied two hundred acres of prime Fraser River benchland replete with staff residences, a stone chapel, gymnasium, carpenter shop, cannery, dairy and horse barns, hen houses, implement sheds, a blacksmith shop, a piggery, and sheep folds.[1] An imposing, three-storey brick building housed dormitories, classrooms, assembly hall, administrative offices, sewing rooms, an infirmary, kitchens, and dining rooms.

1. Ron Purvis, *T'shama* (Surrey: Heritage House, 1994), 8.

Ruby Dunstan lived at St. George's from 1948 to 1953 with 250 other children and a staff of 30 (supervisors, teachers, and farm and dairy managers) under the close watch of the principal and his head matron.[2] In her thank-you speech, she downplayed her own achievements to talk about children. Ruby was one of the first to go public with the horrific abuses against children by employees of St. George's. Journalist Geoffrey York sought her out in the late 1980s for his book *The Dispossessed: Life and Death in Native Canada.* "They treated us like animals," she told him, "and they expected us to come out a happy person. As far as I know, nobody has ever come out of there happy."[3] "You were told you shouldn't be an Indian."[4]

The Dispossessed drew attention to crimes that Ruby brought forward, as Bev does now. In Lytton, seventeen boys, some as young as nine years old, were victimized by a dormitory supervisor over a twelve-year period.[5] Sitting beside us during Ruby's party was band member Charon Spinks. I was a good friend of Charon's mother, Hilda. During our visits, she cried about sending her five well-scrubbed children to the school and having them returned to her for short holidays covered in head lice and telling stories of failed escapes.

Hilda was one of the lucky ones. After the loss of her parents to the 1918 flu, she and her sister, Millie, were sent to live with their grandmother, Sapelle, an Indian doctor. Sapelle took the girls into the back hills of the Okanagan to evade the annual school pickup. "You won't learn anything there," she told them, "and you'll probably end up pregnant."[6] York interviewed Charon about her experience at St. George's from 1950 to 1957 and heard stories like those told by Bev. She was "Number 473," and it is "still burned on her consciousness ...

2. Purvis, 8.
3. Geoffrey York, *The Dispossessed: Life and Death in Native Canada* (Toronto: Lester & Orpen Dennys, 1989), 34.
4. York, 25.
5. York, 28.
6. Wickwire/Austin, recorded interviews in the author's possession.

I've still got scars on my fingers from being whacked with key rings and yardsticks ... I remember crying without tears'.[7]

The old brick school building was torched in 1983, and there were rumours of arson.

In his book *Shingwauk's Vision: A History of Native Residential Schools*, historian Jim Miller listed eighteen "Indian" industrial schools and thirty-six boarding schools in Canada by the end of the nineteenth century[8] with even more in the early twentieth century. Parents who withheld their children faced jail. At the McKenna-McBride Royal Commission's hearings on reserve boundaries, local chiefs tried to shift the conversation to residential schools. At Spences Bridge on November 3, 1913, Chief John Tetlenitsa pleaded instead for a day school on his Cooks Ferry Band land, offering to provide a site for a school and to help build it: "When the children go to a boarding school they are just like being lost to us."[9] Upriver at Kamloops, Tetlenitsa's colleague Chief Louis stated: "I expected to see my people improve when they first went to Industrial School, but I have not seen anything of it."[10]

In fact, these schools were designed to "lose" the children from their home environments. As the Superintendent General of Indian Affairs expressed it in 1889, such schools would isolate the child from "the deleterious home influences to which he would otherwise be subjected ... [and strip him of] the uncivilized state in which he has

7. York, 35.

8. J.R. Miller, *Shingwauk's Vision: A History of Native Residential Schools* (Toronto: University of Toronto Press, 1996), 116.

9. Chief John Tetlenitsa, in a statement before the members of the McKenna-McBride Royal Commission on Indian Affairs for the Province of British Columbia, at Spences Bridge, British Columbia, November 3, 1913. British Columbia Archives, Add. MSS 1056, box 1, file 7.

10. Chief Louis, in a statement before the members of the McKenna-McBride Royal Commission on Indian Affairs for the Province of British Columbia, at Kamloops, as quoted in Celia Haig-Brown, *Resistance and Renewal: Surviving the Residential School* (Vancouver: Arsenal Pulp Press, 1988), 111.

been brought up."[11] Language barriers in the early twentieth century made challenges difficult. According to the ethnographer James Teit, who knew the local people well and spent years advocating on their behalf, "not one in 200 could sign his name" in 1904.[12]

The rise of the North American counterculture in the 1960s opened the door to change. Young people rallied around the American Civil Rights Movement and Vietnam War protests, inspiring other campaigns for human rights and social justice. The American Indian Movement and books like Vine Deloria Jr.'s *Custer Died for Your Sins: An Indian Manifesto* helped inspire a new generation of Indian leaders.[13] In Canada, these leaders (including Bev's partner, Bill Wilson) found ample justification for protest: the 1969 White Paper, the James Bay hydroelectric project, and the Mackenzie Valley pipeline. These protests culminated in demands for the inclusion of Aboriginal rights in the Canadian constitution. George Ryga's *The Ecstasy of Rita Joe* premiered at the Vancouver Playhouse in 1967 and exposed settler Canadians to the realities of Indigenous life in the city. The 1970s saw large land-claims cases such as the now-famous *Calder* case, and the launch of new Native studies programs.

During these years, Indigenous elders – primarily women now fluent in English – began telling their stories to outsiders. In the Yukon, Angela Sidney, Kitty Smith, and Annie Ned told their life stories to Julie Cruikshank.[14] Mrs. Sidney, notes Cruikshank, "understood that family members wanted her to record the story of her life and that I was a willing secretary and an eager student, [but] she had very clear

11. Quoted in Elizabeth Furniss, *Victims of Benevolence: The Dark Legacy of the Williams Lake Indian Residential School* (Vancouver: Arsenal Pulp Press, 1995), 27.

12. Letter, James Teit to Franz Boas, March 10, 1904. Boas Professional Correspondence, The Library, American Philosophical Society, Philadelphia.

13. Vine Deloria Jr., *Custer Died for Your Sins: An Indian Manifesto* (Norman: University of Oklahoma Press, 1969).

14. Julie Cruikshank (in collaboration with Angela Sidney, Kitty Smith, and Annie Ned), *Life Lived Like a Story: Life Stories of Three Yukon Native Elders* (Lincoln: University of Nebraska Press, 1990).

ideas about how we should proceed."[15] In southern British Columbia, Nlaka'pamux elder Annie York told her story to Andrea Laforet; Haida elder Florence Davidson told hers to Margaret Blackman; and Mary John, Carrier elder from Stoney Creek, told hers to Bridget Moran.[16]

Okanagan elder Harry Robinson explained to me that he wanted to record the many stories he had accumulated over his lifetime: "I'm going to disappear and there'll be no more telling stories ... You can still hear that when I'm dead ... And think and look and try and look ahead and look around at the stories."[17] As anthropologist Carole McGranahan wrote recently, "Narrating one's life ... is to situate oneself and to be situated in dialogue with society."[18] And, in Robinson's mind, there was need for dialogue with society. Whites, he explained, needed to know the "Indian" side of the story of land theft and colonialism.

Some of these elderly narrators highlighted the racism and inequality that came with White colonization. Others – Julie Cruikshank's hosts, Mrs. Sidney; Margaret Blackman's host, Florence Davidson; and some of my hosts (such as Aimee August) – recounted their past with eloquence, but bracketed the negativity.

In *They Called Me Number One*, Bev Sellars chronicles the experiences of a third generation, the grandchildren of the 1960s elders. Like the Nlaka'pamux families within the reach of St. George's, Bev's Secwepemc family members were captured by the St. Joseph's Mission established upriver in 1886 by the Oblates of Mary Immaculate, a

---

15. Cruikshank, 24.
16. Andrea Laforet and Annie York, *Spuzzum: Fraser Canyon Histories, 1808–1939* (Vancouver: University of British Columbia Press, 1998); Margaret Blackman, *During My Time: Florence Edenshaw Davidson, a Haida Woman* (Vancouver: Greystone, 1982); Bridget Moran, *Stoney Creek Woman: The Story of Mary John* (Vancouver: Arsenal Pulp Press, 1997).
17. Wickwire/Robinson, recorded interview in the author's possession.
18. Carole McGranahan, "Narrative Dispossession: Tibet and the Gendered Logistics of Historical Possibility," *Comparative Studies in Society and History* 52, 4 (2010): 768.

French order of the Roman Catholic church.[19] There was no escape. Her "Gram" (Sarah Baptiste Sam), born in 1896, spent ten years at the school and then saw her children and grandchildren follow suit, with Bev's mother, Evelyn Sellars, attending St. Joseph's Mission for ten years beginning in 1931 at age six, and Bev attending for five years beginning in 1962 at age seven. The school closed in 1981. Like St. George's, it was under police investigation at the time for extreme offences against children.

I met Bev in the late 1990s. She had already served for six years as chief of the Soda Creek Band, and was finishing her bachelor of arts in history at the University of Victoria. Like Ruby Dunstan, Bev had worked to bring to light the Williams Lake school story. In June 1991, she gave the opening speech at the First National Conference on Residential Schools.[20] Last spring, Bev sent me her book manuscript, and I couldn't put it down. I had read many elders' life histories and residential-school accounts and followed the proceedings of the Truth and Reconciliation Commission of Canada.

Yet Bev gives us something new – a tale told through *five* generations more than a century, from grandmother to grandchildren. Though a story of pain, it is told with grace and composure. A gifted storyteller, Bev takes us all on a journey that, by the end, feels strangely uplifting.

This book is filled with images that stay with the reader – like the *Lord of the Flies* scenario that erupts when one child is given new shoes while the others get hand-me-downs; or the brutal humiliations inflicted on young runaways; or the grandparents who were denied details of a grandchild's illness. I still feel the power of Bev's Gram, who made sure that her grandchild in her cabin in the woods was

19. For an excellent study of the history of this school, see Elizabeth Furniss, *Victims of Benevolence: The Dark Legacy of the Williams Lake Indian Residential School* (Vancouver: Arsenal Pulp Press, 1992).
20. The full transcript of Bev Sellars's speech can be found in Elizabeth Furniss's *Victims of Benevolence*, 121–28.

raised with the values that would carry her through the world of racism and oppression that she knew she would face.

I read this book with tears and laughter, frowns and smiles, anger and joy. I stand in awe and appreciation.

Notes

My Grandmother and Others Before Me

While doing research in the Victoria, British Columbia archives, I found out that Frank Guy's estate was sold after his death and that all money went to his family in France.

While doing research in the archives in Ottawa, I found the transcript for Mom's trial. My blood boiled when I read about the fat, ugly man bragging to others about what he was going to do with Mom after he had gotten them drunk. All the people he told about his plans for Mom came forward to testify on Mom and Michel's behalf. She and her husband, Michel, were acquitted of the murder.

NOTES ON CHAPTER 2
Sardis Hospital = Loneliness

Too many stories about Sardis Hospital don't make sense. There are accusations that the hospitals used some of the Aboriginal patients as guinea pigs for experiments of one sort or another. One family in my community, the Michels, remembers two brothers and a sister taken away. One brother spent six years there from the time he was six months old until he was six years old. The other brother was five when they took him and was thirteen when he came home. The girl was at the hospital for two years. One boy from a neighbouring community spent ten years at the hospital. He was sixteen when he went home and he did not know anyone. He was so used to hospital life he couldn't handle his community, which was going through one of its darkest periods ever. He ended up committing suicide the same summer he went home. Another girl who I got to know at Sardis and who I later went to school with at the Mission denied up and down that she had ever been at Sardis. She threatened me with physical violence when I insisted that she was with me there. I left her alone, but I still wonder why she refused to admit she was in hospital. Her family later confirmed that she had been there. My grandparents were at the hospital for eight months. The Indian nurse and the Indian agent required them to go there. Gram couldn't understand why they had to go to hospital because they were healthy. They had to turn over their pension cheques to the people at the hospital and Gram said they received no medical treatment. Eventually, she talked her way into having them released. Gram said it was not easy to persuade the doctors to let them go even though they were not receiving treatment. Because they were status Indians, they needed permission before they could leave. Institutions of all sorts were used as a method of control over Aboriginal people.

NOTES ON CHAPTER 3

St. Joseph's Mission = Prison

I found a letter in the archives from the Department of Indian Affairs to the school during the period when my mom attended advising the school that getting the children to wash their sheets once a month was not enough and stressing that it should be done more often.

I also found letters about the cold weather in the winter and the difficulty in heating the buildings. One letter during the years my mom was at the Mission talked about the temperature in the dormitory being a few degrees below freezing during the night.

Letters in the archives releasing students from the schools use only numbers. The following is an example of one I found: "January 27, 1951 Mr. R.J. Meek Supt. Indian Agency Whitehorse, Y.T. The department approves the discharge of the following pupils from the Carcross Indian Residential School. No. 167 183 0154 0186 Philip Phelan Chief, Education Division."

NOTES ON CHAPTER 4

I Get Religion But What Did It Mean?

About the restriction on Gram's use of her language at the Mission, the suppression of the Aboriginal languages across Canada for more than one hundred years has definitely taken its toll. In my community, the only people who speak our language fluently are those who came here from other Secwepemc communities. All of our fluent speakers are dead. In some communities, there are no fluent speakers anymore. Canada says they have two official languages, English and French, and once again the original inhabitants of this land are ignored. Many Aboriginal people feel there should be at least one of the many Aboriginal languages recognized as an official language.

As for the labour we did while at the Mission, while doing research at the archives, I ran across some letters from businessmen in Williams Lake in the 1930s who wanted the government to do something about the free labour that the Mission had in the children. The businessmen did not complain about the use of child labour or the treatment of the children. They complained that they had to pay their workers and couldn't compete with the Mission, which sold harnesses, tack, vegetables, and other goods that the kids produced.

NOTES ON CHAPTER 7

Pain, Bullying, But Also Pleasure

Funerals are a way of life for Aboriginal people. I have been to hundreds of funerals. Many funerals I have been to are not because I know the person who has died but I might know his or her daughter, granddaughter, niece. We go to comfort and support each other, and I did not realize how supportive we were of each other until I attended a funeral at Sugar Cane led by a visiting priest, someone who worked only with the church in Williams Lake. His congregation would have been mostly White. When it was time for the eulogy, the priest decided to say a few words because one had not been prepared. The person who had died was a street person in Williams Lake, yet the priest commented that this person would be greatly missed because so many people had attended his funeral. I looked around and realized that because this priest was used to just a few people at non-Aboriginal funerals, he probably thought that the crowd of about one hundred was a huge funeral. In fact, it was a small funeral, and I was feeling bad for the family because there were not many people there. I have seen many Aboriginal funerals where five hundred or more attended. Aboriginal people have a common understanding of pain and suffering, and we understand why there are so many tragic deaths. Our communities are always there to try to pick up the pieces as best we can for those who are left to mourn. Funerals are a time to support the family, but they are also a time to reconnect with others from neighbouring communities and tribes. All differences are put aside and everyone comes together as one.

NOTES ON CHAPTER 8

Home Sweet Home

The report of the Commission of Inquiry concerning the Adequacy of Compensation Paid to Donald Marshall, Jr., is a good reference point for the programming we got at residential school. Marshall was a Mi'kmaq Indian who spent eleven years in jail for a crime he did not commit. The types of losses that a person suffers as a result of wrongful imprisonment were identified in a paper by Professor H. Archibald Kaiser. Anyone who attended residential school can easily identify with the same losses: loss of liberty; loss of reputation; humiliation and disgrace; pain and suffering; loss of enjoyment of life; loss of potential normal experiences; other foregone developmental experiences, such as education or social learning in the normal workplace; loss of civil rights; loss of social intercourse with friends, neighbours, and family; physical assaults while in prison by fellow inmates and staff; subjection to prison discipline, including extraordinary punishments imposed legally; accepting and adjusting to prison life, knowing it was all unjustly imposed; adverse effects on the claimant's future, specifically the prospects of marriage, social status, physical and mental health and social relations generally. Professor Kaiser continues with an apt commentary:

> Surely few people need to be told that imprisonment in general has very serious social and psychological effects on the inmate. For the wrongfully convicted person, this harm is heightened, as it is hardly possible for the sane innocent person to accept not only the inevitability but the injustice of that which is imposed upon him. For the person who has been subjected to a lengthy term of imprisonment, we approach the worst-case scenario. The notion of permanent social disability due to a state wrong begins to crystallize. The longer this distorting experience of prison goes on, the less likely a person can ever be whole again. Especially for the individual imprisoned as a youth, the chances of eventual happy integration into the community must be very slim.

The report goes on to say that evidence reveals that prisoners live without privacy, subject to rules that govern their every hour – a life without freedom, without hope, and without dignity. Another comment by Professor Kaiser was that "there is no dollar figure which can replace lost years, lost opportunities or compensate for the injury sustained by the victim." Now you take all of that and put children, some as young as four and five years old, in the same conditions and one can easily see why the schools were so devastating to our communities.

Indian agents, priests, Indian nurses, and the RCMP had control over every aspect of our lives. In the 1950s, Doreen (Bates) Sellars and her sister, Lena Bowe, who were both married to non-status Indians, went to visit their mom, Annie Sellars, on the Soda Creek reserve. Having non-status husbands made Doreen and Lena non-status as well. Everyone saw that their skin hadn't become lighter, and they did not otherwise appear different but, by virtue of the Indian Act, they were no longer "Indian." The Department of Indian Affairs made it law that only "Indians" were allowed on Indian reserves. Even though they were born and raised at Soda Creek, Doreen and Lena were breaking the law by visiting their mom. They were trespassing.

Old Antoine Peeps, the chief at the time, who had a personal grudge against that family, informed the Indian agent that Doreen and Lena were on the reserve. The Indian agent came and kicked Doreen and Lena off. My auntie Annie sent a message to her son, Percy Sellars, at Lyons Ranch where he worked. Percy went and got his sisters and then went to the Indian agent and told him that he was taking Doreen and Lena to his place on the Deep Creek reserve. Percy also told the Indian agent that he had better not try to kick his sisters off the reserve from his place. He told the agent that his sisters were born and raised in the community and had every right to be there. Doreen and Lena were not bothered after that. The discriminatory provisions of the Indian Act stayed in place until 1985, when amendments brought the act into line with provisions of the Canadian Charter of Rights and Freedoms.

My uncles and brothers found it easier to hide from the authority figures rather than confront them. A cop car coming meant trouble coming. I hated those times. There was always a feeling of being intruded upon when someone would say, "Cops" or "Priest" or "The Nurse" or "The Indian Agent." Zoom! Like magic, everyone pulled a disappearing act. Up the stairs or out the back door they went. They would hide until they were sure the coast was clear. I learned at a very young age that it was "them against us." Canadian society with their courts, the politicians with their legislation, and society in general all upheld these racist laws and policies against Aboriginal people.

The Catholic church wanted complete control of our lives from the time we were born to the time we died. Our parents went to church and did other things the Catholic church dictated because of the fear instilled in them since childhood which was used to control their adult lives. If anyone died without being baptized, they were not allowed to be buried in the graveyard where the rest of our community members were buried. Ellen Michel was one of my grandmother's closest friends. They were so close that Ellen, my grandmother, and Gram's sister, Annie, called each other sisters. They weren't blood related at all, but they chose to think of themselves as sisters. A few years before Ellen died, in 1990, she was over visiting Gram. She was talking about her baby that had to be buried in their field at Deep Creek all by itself. There was a small fence around the grave but, over the years, it has deteriorated. Ellen and her husband, Louie, didn't have enough time to baptize the baby before it died. The priest assigned to our community would not allow the baby to be buried in our graveyard because the baby died shortly after birth and had not yet been baptized! So, according to Catholic "law" this innocent little baby was not "pure" enough to be buried with the ones who had been baptized. It was banished from our community graveyard by the priest. Sixty years later, Ellen was still deeply hurt by it. Her granddaughter, Barb Dixon, said Ellen worried about the baby and talked about it a lot. According to the priest, in order for anyone to go to heaven they first had to be baptized. This little baby wasn't baptized, and Ellen worried about where its spirit ended up. I assume she feared the worst based on the teachings of the Church. How could these priests be so cold-hearted as to condemn a little soul like that as an outcast from our community and not allow the mother the comfort of thinking her relatives who had already passed on into the spirit world would look after her little one? The hypocrisy of the Catholic church never ceases to amaze me. On one hand, they preach that we are all "God's children," and on the other hand they condemn an innocent little baby who never had a chance to commit any sin except dying before it was baptized.

Sometimes I still get such an intense hatred for the people and policies that so negatively affected my family and fellow "Indians." I try not to think about it too much because I know that it will eat away at me inside. I don't want to go back to living my life with such anger most of the time. It is important to remember these things, but I can't let the anger rule my life.

When I was fourteen or fifteen years old, I was at Soda Creek in my mom and Lawrence's house when a female relative came in. She had blood smeared on her throat and a cut under one eye, not a big one but enough to make it bleed. She was pretty shook up. She had been hitchhiking home from town and a White guy driving a hydro service truck picked her up. They got to the airport turnoff, eight miles north of Williams Lake, and he said he just had to go up there for a few minutes to fix something and then he would run her home. She believed him. He took her on a deserted road, got out, and came around to her side of the truck. He threw her out of the truck and was going to rape her. After throwing her down on the ground he saw she had her menstrual period. He swore at her and then took his knife out. He held it to her face and gave her a knick on the face just below her eye and the other on her throat. He said that if she ever told anyone, he would find her and cut out her eye and slit her throat open. He left her there on the ground, got in his truck, and drove away. She fixed herself up and walked down to the highway. She would not hitchhike again. She began to walk the fifteen or so miles home. People from our community who were coming from town eventually picked her up.

Even though it would have been easy for her to identify the hydro man, reporting it to the police was not an option. We knew it would be a useless exercise, and more trouble would follow if we reported it. Judging from past experiences when White men raped Native women, she would probably have been made to look like a whore in court, and the guy would probably have been acquitted. That was common knowledge in the Aboriginal community. The White man would have denied it, and that would have been the end of it. That was the way it was and, some would argue, still is. When I was eighteen, I was living at Soda Creek. I was home alone. A cop came to the door and was looking for a lady who was living with one of our men. Apparently, there had been a death in her family and the RCMP had been asked to find her. There were few phones in the Aboriginal communities at the time, so if the RCMP were looking for someone, they had to make a trip out to Soda Creek. I told the cop that Cynthia and Tom lived out at Fish Lake. There was a training centre set up out there at the time. While he was talking to me he was looking past me into my house. Finally, he asked me if I was alone. I said yes. I thought he might think Cynthia was with me. He asked if he could come in. Alarm bells went off immediately. I said no. He then asked me if I could go with him out to Fish Lake. I again told him no. He said he didn't know where Fish Lake was and could I show him? I knew damn well he knew where Fish Lake was. It had a reputation for trouble, and the RCMP were constantly being called there. He kept trying to convince me to go with him. Even though he was an officer of the "law," and I should have had no reason to fear him, my Aboriginal experiences immediately put up huge red flags not to get in that car with him. I knew the laws for his people and the laws for my people were not the same. Once I realized what he was trying to do, I stepped out of the house so that we would be in full view of the other community members. He finally left. I heard later that an RCMP officer had sexually assaulted an Aboriginal girl from a neighbouring community after he lured her into his car. It was about the same time as my encounter with the RCMP officer. The girl reported it, but they refused to believe her. Nothing happened after that.

At Soda Creek, all the houses were built in a circle, and a road went around the reserve. During the spring and summer months we had at least one car a week and sometimes several cars a week filled with White people driving around the reserve. They would, of course, have their windows rolled up and their doors locked as they slowly drove around the reserve. They were not ashamed to gawk. We all hated their uninvited intrusion into our little neck of the woods. It was easy to identify the gawkers because they usually drove cars that Aboriginal people at the time would not be able to afford. At first, I would just go in the house when I saw an unfamiliar car coming around the reserve. Later on, I got so sick of it and would just glare at them. Once I got an unloaded gun, stood on my porch, and held the gun by my side so they could see it. I was looking right at them. The car went zooming out of the reserve. I expected the cops to come out after a complaint was laid, but they never did.

NOTES ON CHAPTER 11

One Day I Realized I Had Survived

Many Aboriginal girls lost their babies through forced adoption, and many were later forced to give up their children to foster care. The "Sixties Scoop" refers to the adoption of Aboriginal children in Canada when children were literally scooped from their homes and communities. Government authorities and social workers acted under the continued racist assumption that Aboriginal people were inferior and unfit to raise their own children. Even though this practice went on well past the 1960s and into the 1970s, the highest numbers of adoptions took place in the 1960s. In many ways, it is still happening today.

Unfortunately, far too many Aboriginal youth do not make it. According to the Canadian Mental Health Association, "Suicide and self-injury were the leading causes of death for Aboriginal youths. In 2000, suicide accounted for 22 percent of all deaths among Aboriginal youth (aged 10 to 19 years) and 16 percent of all deaths among Aboriginal people aged 20 to 44 years." It also says that, "Suicide rates of Registered Indian youths (aged 15 to 24) are eight times higher than the national rate for females and five times higher than the national rate for males."

My brother Ray died in the Williams Lake hospital one night in 1977. He was only thirty-two years old. Ray had always complained about his heart. He would say, "I think I'm having a heart attack." We would laugh because he seemed so healthy, and we would tease him and tell him he was just hungover. Native people rarely went to the doctor those days unless it was to see Dr. Lee, the only Chinese doctor in town. Gram did not seek the services of a doctor until she was eighty-eight years old. She had such tremendous pain in her knee, she finally agreed to seek help. All her experiences with doctors had been negative. She was still bitter when she told me of her daughter Janet who died when she was only twelve years old. Janet suffered with severe headaches and the Indian medicines did not help, so Gram, in desperation, went to see a doctor in Williams Lake. Gram said she was so upset when the doctor told Gram that the only thing the matter with Janet was that Gram gave her too much coffee. Gram did not allow her kids to drink coffee. She took Janet home, but the headaches got so bad Gram had to take her to the hospital. Janet ended up dying during the night. The next day, Gram went back to the hospital and they told her that her daughter was dead because of a brain tumour. The girl in the bed next to Janet told Gram that no one did anything for Janet. Apparently, they had not even given her Aspirin for her headaches. Gram always felt guilty and angry for leaving Janet in the hospital. She said that if Janet were home, at least she would have attended to her and tried to make her comfortable. She hated that Janet died in pain and with no one around to comfort her. Gram also had a son who had a hunchback. Gram treated him at home but he died at the age of twenty-two years. Mom later asked the community nurses what the hunchback would have been caused by, and they told her tuberculosis.

Following in that tradition, Ray did not go see a doctor and ended up dying of a massive heart attack. It was my job to go and tell Gram and my uncle Johnny about Ray's death. Ray died in December, and it was so cold, forty degrees below zero, that they could not finish burying him. The dirt that should have been returned to the grave had frozen solid, and the workers could not loosen it to bury Ray. They managed to put half the dirt into the grave before they got too cold to continue. This was the only time I have seen a coffin sit by a grave until the next day.

There was an independent inquiry into Ray's death. Apparently someone, probably someone who worked in the hospital, felt that there was negligence in his treatment. We only found out about the inquiry because it was on the Kamloops TV news. I was surprised to hear about the inquiry, but the only thing I thought was that Ray would have been "tickled pink" to hear his name on the TV news. He once was in an advertisement for the Williams Lake Stampede, and he thought that was the greatest thing in the world. At a previous stampede parade there was a mechanical bull on wheels. Ray, who had been drinking, went over and asked the guy if he could ride the mechanical bull. Ray fancied himself a bull rider, but I don't think he did very well in rodeos. He wore a cowboy hat and, when he got on the mechanical bull, someone videotaped him. They used the video as an advertisement for the stampede. Every time the advertisement came on TV, he would beam with pride.

So, from the TV news we found out that there might have been some negligent medical treatment when Ray died. No one felt the need to inform his family of what, who, or why there was an inquiry. We were not informed of when or where it would be, and so no one attended. No one contacted us with the results of the inquiry. Of course, our programming taught us not to ask questions. Just accept.

About fifteen years later, my mom was talking about Ray's death. She asked me to try to find out what had happened in the hospital and why Ray had died. I found out who to write to and asked for the results of that inquiry. I got a very short letter that said the inquiry found no one at the hospital at fault. There was no explanation and no insight into why an inquiry had taken place. I left it at that for the same reason we did not ask about it in the first place.

NOTES ON CHAPTER 14

Final Thoughts

In 2004, the Aboriginal Healing Foundation released a number of reports on the effects of colonization and the residential schools. The *Historic Trauma and Aboriginal Healing* booklet indicates that Medieval Europe had similar experiences and responses, such as rampant alcoholism, social instability, cultural and moral break-down, spiritual rejection, as well as profound mental and emotional withdrawal from the trauma of hundreds of years of bubonic plagues and the social disruption that followed. The booklet goes on to say that comparison with European experiences during and after the plagues helps to illustrate that, once traumatic events stop for a sufficient length of time – research says it takes forty years – before socio-cultural reconstruction and healing will begin.

The booklet goes on to say that Aboriginal people still don't have the forty years needed to recover. For the past five hundred years, entire Aboriginal communities have been continuously trauma-tized by the millions and millions of deaths from diseases brought by non-Aboriginals, expulsion from their homelands, loss of economic, and self-sufficiency, removal of children from their homes, assimi-lation tactics, and incarceration in prisons and residential schools. The trauma of colonialism is still happening today. Although not as ubiquitous as it was before, it is still there. All the social problems in Aboriginal communities are not because we are "Indians." The prob-lem is a *human* problem and a result of hundreds of years of trauma.

Index

A

Abbey, Alice 70
Aboriginal Healing
  Foundation 213
Aboriginal medicine. *See* health
  and healing
abuse
  emotional 45, 50, 87, 88, 90,
    99, 111, 121, 145, 174, 181,
    185, 204, 212
  physical 11, 33, 34, 37, 39,
    43–45, 47, 48, 61–63, 85–87,
    96, 97, 99, 112, 122, 127, 133,
    140, 159, 195
  sexual 40, 47, 65, 93, 98, 99
  verbal 26, 49, 67, 81, 82, 104,
    112, 126, 140, 150, 168, 173,
    174
acceptable touching 17, 31, 52,
  76, 89–92, 181
adoption, forced 147, 210
adverse effects of residential
  school experience
  anxiety and panic attacks 112,
    124
  self-hatred 111, 181
agriculture
  hay cutting 51, 107
  livestock 31, 61, 105, 108, 201
  vegetable gardening 49, 51,
    61, 94
air cadets. *See* military service
alcohol and drugs 181
  alcoholism 39, 89, 180, 213
  as coping mechanism 31, 181
  bootlegging 134, 135
  alec (kinnikinnick) 55, 57

Alec, Ellie 44
Alec, Willie 37, 70
Alexandria 3
Alexis, Lucy (Jimmie) 96, 97
Alkali Lake 142, 163
ambulance response times 63,
  64, 120, 121
American Civil Rights
  Movement 196
American Indian Movement 196
Amut, Chris 70, 153
Amut, Lorna (Boyce) 88, 89
Archie, Arlene 70
Archie, Danny 70, 76
Archie, Ernest 70
Archie, Lyle John 70
Archie, Nancy 36, 88, 89, 116,
  117
Aucoin, Cyril 87, 91

B

Baptiste, John (Guy) 3, 5
Baptiste, Marguerite 4
Baptiste, Old Twan 3, 5
Baptiste, Sarah 3, 6, 7, 9, 14, 15,
  68, 198
Barkerville 4, 9, 10
Basil, Sarah Jane 7, 9
Beautiful British Columbia
  (1940) 81
Beaver Lake 5
Beaver Valley 3
bedbugs 13
bedwetting 33, 63
Bella Coola 115
Belleau, Dave 163

L

labour and child labour. *See* chores
LaCeese, Cecilia   51
Lac La Hache   80
Laforet, Andrea   197
land, Aboriginal relationship to   3,
   16, 17, 57, 108, 138
languages
   English   13, 15, 44, 45, 118, 119,
     130, 183, 196, 203
   First Nation   44
   French   45, 130, 198, 203
Laurant, Mable   96
lawyers and law firms   166–169, 175
Lee, Dr. (Williams Lake)   211
letters and correspondence,
   censorship of   68
lice. *See* head lice
life on the street   184
livestock   31, 51, 61, 108
loans, personal   39
logging camps   147, 148, 152
loneliness   23–25, 34, 151
Loretta, Sister   66
loss and the residential school
   experience   204
Lulua, James   70, 78
Lyons Ranch   206
Lytton Band   193, 194

M

Mack, Dayton   138–142, 147, 148,
   152, 155, 156, 159, 160
Mackenzie Valley pipeline   196
Mack, Jacinda   45, 145–148, 160,
   183
Mack, Orden   61, 95, 161
Mack, Scott   146–148, 160, 183
Mack, Tony, Jr.   147, 148
Mack, Tony, Sr.   147
manual labour   35, 51, 53, 57, 64,
   94, 104, 105, 123, 139
Marguerite   3–5, 7
Mary (great-grandmother)   3
McGranahan, Carole   197
McIsaac, Mr.   38, 39
McKenna-McBride Royal
   Commission   195
Meares Island   187
medical care and treatment. *See*
   health and healing
Meek, R.J.   202
Meldrum Creek   131
Meldrum, Leona   130, 131
memory, repressed   36, 40
menstruation   108, 208
mental abuse   45, 50, 87, 88, 90,
   99, 111, 121, 145, 174, 181, 185,
   204, 212
M'Gonigle, Michael   193
Michel, Ellen   207
Michel, Reg   70
Mi'kmaq   204
military service   14
Miller, Jim: *Shingwauk's Vision*
   (1996)   166, 185, 195

physical abuse   11, 33, 34, 37, 39,
    43–45, 47, 48, 61–63, 85–87,
    96, 97, 99, 112, 122, 127, 133,
    140, 159, 195
physical affection   90, 181
Place, Hilary   116
play
    bows and arrows   94, 104, 105
    card games   103
    ice skating   77, 79
    ice tag   77
    playhouses   55
    riding in tires   79
    sledding   102, 103
    swings   73
Point, Steven   190
police. *See* Royal Canadian
    Mounted Police
politics
    Aboriginal   163, 171, 183, 187
    non-Aboriginal   184
Pop, David   70, 80
Pop, Margaret (Mop)   137
Pop, Rick   80
Porter, June (Sellars)   57
prayers and praying   32, 43, 110
prehospital trauma-related
    death   63, 64, 120, 121
Presley, Elvis   82
priests, brothers, and nuns. *See*
    nuns, brothers, and priests
priests, Father O'Connor   54, 63,
    64, 87, 91–93, 97, 111, 123, 124
Prince George College   136
prison and jail   10, 17, 164, 182,
    204, 205
privacy   29, 205

programming and indoctrina-
    tion   45, 87, 90, 121, 145,
    174, 185
property rights. *See Calder v. British
    Columbia (Attorney General)*
public schools   86, 127, 131
punishment and discipline
    bread and water   59
    head shaving   96
    kneeling   38, 43, 44, 65, 96
    strapping   33, 34, 39, 43–45,
    47, 48, 61–63, 85–87, 96, 97,
    112, 159

Q

Quesnel   3, 7, 89
Quesnel Band   89
Quilt, Jerry   70

R

racism and oppression   145, 189,
    197, 199
    laws and policies   206
Ranch Café (Williams Lake)   157
reading   87, 89, 154, 158, 190
reconciliation and healing   170,
    189, 213
recreation
    ice skating   77, 79
    riding in tires   79
    walks   55, 57
regalia and dancing, restrictions
    against   157
report cards   111
Report on the Cariboo-Chilcotin
    Justice Inquiry   169
repressed memory   36, 40